Praying with Our Lady of Guadalupe

Dan Lynch

Copyright 2006

Copyright © 2006 Dan Lynch

All rights reserved. this book may not be published or in any way reproduced in whole or in part, stored in a retrieval system, or transmitted, in any form or by any means, electronic, mechanical, photocopying, recording, or otherwise, without written permission. Please do no copy without permission.

Published by:
JKMI Press
144 Sheldon Road
St. Albans, VT 05478
www.JKMI.com

ISBN 0-9647988-8-3

Contents

An Introduction to Prayer	1
The Story of Our Lady of Guadalupe	5
The Missionary Image of Our Lady of Guadalupe and Visitations	7
Pope John Paul II's Prophesies for Our Lady of Guadalupe	9
Pope John Paul II's Entrustment of the New Evangelization of America to Our Lady of Guadalupe	10
Our Lady of Guadalupe and the Gospel of Life	13
Opening Prayer for the Mass of Our Lady of Guadalupe	16
Words of Our Lady of Guadalupe to Saint Juan Diego and to You	17
Pope John Paul II's Prayers	19
Act of Consecration to Our Lady of Guadalupe	19
For a Pilgrimage of Mary in America	21
For the Church in America through Our Lady of Guadalupe	21
For the Sick of America through Our Lady of Guadalupe	24
For Peace through Our Lady of Guadalupe	25
For Life to Mary, Bright Dawn of the New World	27
For the Families of America through Our Lady of Guadalupe	29
To Saint Juan Diego	30
Prayers of Other Popes with Our Lady of Guadalupe	33

Meditations with Our Lady of Guadalupe on the Mysteries of the Rosary	35
The Joyful Mysteries	36
The Luminous Mysteries	38
The Sorrowful Mysteries	40
The Glorious Mysteries	42
U.S. Bishops' Novena to Our Lady of Guadalupe, Patroness of All America	44
The Way of the Cross with Our Lady of Guadalupe	47
Introduction	48
Preface and Opening Scripture	59
Opening Prayer	61
The Stations of the Cross	64
Closing Prayer for Unborn Victims	92
Concluding Station Prayers	95
The Chaplet of Our Lady of Guadalupe	98
Memorare to Our Lady of Guadalupe	100
Make of Me a Tilma	101
Act of Consecration and Crowning to Our Lady of Guadalupe, Patroness and Protectress of the Unborn	102

Mexican Bishops' and Basilica's Prayers for Missionary Image of Our Lady of Guadalupe	106
Act of Consecration to Our Lady of Guadalupe by Archbishop John Donoghue before Missionary Image	108
Prayers for Life with Our Lady of Guadalupe	110
Introduction	111
The Prayer Service	118
The Prologue - The Word of God	119
Power and Authority Over Satan	121
The Sentence Imposed Upon Satan	121
The Execution of the Sentence	122
Pope Leo XIII's Prayer to Saint Michael the Archangel	131
The Canticles of Elizabeth and Mary	134
Act of Consecration of Guardians of Life	135
Songs to Our Lady of Guadalupe	137
An Inspired Plea from Our Lady of Guadalupe	143
Declaration of Human Life	146
Dan Lynch Productions	150
Order Form	151

An Introduction to Prayer

Prayer is the raising of our minds and hearts to God or the requesting of good things from Him from a humble and contrite heart, the hidden center of our being. (*Catechism of the Catholic Church, (CCC)* 2559). One of His disciples asked Jesus, "Lord teach us to pray." (Lk.11:1). Jesus didn't give him a long explanation. He just prayed out loud and said, "When you pray, this is what to say." Then He taught them the Lord's Prayer.

In the Lord's Prayer we petition God for the holiness of His name, the coming of His kingdom, the fulfillment of His will, the nourishment of our lives, the forgiveness of our sins and our deliverance from temptation and evil.

Prayer expressions are vocal, meditative or contemplative. (*CCC* 2699).Vocal prayer is prayer of words said aloud or silently in our minds such as the Lord's Prayer or the Hail Mary prayer.

Meditative prayer is a quest of the mind to understand the why and how of the Christian life. Mediation engages thought, imagination, emotion and desire. Christian prayer tries above all to meditate on the mysteries of Christ. (*CCC* 2708). For example, we can pray the Rosary by imagining the mystery, placing ourselves as a participant in it, reflecting on its meaning or message and have a silent interior dialogue with God.

Contemplative prayer is a quest from the heart for God alone. It is a gift that we can predispose ourselves to receive in silence by quieting our minds and interior thoughts until we reach silent communion with God in humble faith beyond the senses. It is a gaze of faith fixed on Jesus, attentive to the Word of God in silent love. (*CCC* 2724). The prayers of this book may be prayed in all three expressions.

Why should we pray?

We should pray because God asks this of us. He tirelessly calls each of us to this mysterious encounter with Himself. Prayer unfolds throughout the whole history of salvation as a reciprocal call between God and man. (*CCC* 2591).

We should pray so that we aren't put to the test. Jesus said, "Pray that you may not be put to the test. The spirit is willing but the flesh is weak." (Mk. 14:38).

Where should we pray?

Jesus often retired to deserted places and prayed. (See Lk. 5:16). He also said, "When you pray, go to your private room, shut yourself in and pray to your Father who is in that secret place, and your Father who sees all that is done in secret will reward you." (Mt. 6:5-6).

However, Jesus didn't mean to limit our places of prayer to deserted places and our private rooms. We can pray anywhere from the depths of our hearts. Jesus didn't mean "your private room" only literally but also metaphorically as the room of our heart, the center of our being. Above all we should pray in the church, which is the proper place for liturgical prayer for the parish community and the privileged place for Eucharistic adoration. (*CCC* 2691).

To **whom** should we pray?

We should pray to the Lord Jesus. Even though prayer is primarily addressed to the Father, we should invoke the name of Jesus by the power of the Holy Spirit. We pray in communion with the Blessed Virgin Mary because of her singular cooperation with the Holy Spirit. In this way, we magnify with her the great things the Lord has done for her and entrust our petitions and praises to her. (*CCC* 2680-2682).

For **whom** should we pray?

We should pray for everyone in need and especially for those who persecute us. (See Mt. 5:44). Jesus set the example for us and prayed, "Father forgive them, they know not what they do." (Lk. 23:34).

When should we pray?

We should pray constantly (see 1 Thess. 5:16-17) and at all times in the Spirit. (Eph. 6:18). If we get tired, we should remember that Jesus often prayed all night. (See Lk.6:12).
"We have not been commanded to work, to keep watch and to fast constantly, but it has been laid down that we are to pray without ceasing." (1 Thess 5:17). We should pray especially at turning points in our lives. Jesus set the example and prayed when He chose the twelve to assist Him in His mission and when He entered into His passion.

How should we pray?

We should pray as a person speaks to a friend. Moses spoke to the Lord face to face as a man speaks to his friend. (See Ex. 33:11). We should pray with the right heart in humility like the tax collector and not self-righteously like the Pharisee. (See Lk.18:9-14). We should pray with the Spirit who prays within us (see Rm. 8:26); with our minds and spirits (see 1 Cor.14); with a right heart (see Acts 8:21-22); imploringly (see Lk.11); and without losing heart (see Lk.18:1).
Jesus taught His parable on praying with persistence to obtain loaves of bread from a friend for an unexpected guest. (See Lk.11). He taught us not to lose heart, but to pray always like the widow to the corrupt judge. (See Lk.18:1).

What intentions should we pray for?

We should pray in praise of God, in adoration of Him, in contrition for offending Him, in thanksgiving for Him and in petition to Him, especially for the coming of His Kingdom. We should pray for mercy (see Lk.8); for healing (see James 13:16); and for unity (see Jn.17). We should pray in intercession for the needs of others, especially for those who persecute us. (See Mt. 5:44). These general forms of prayer are explained in the *Catechism of the Catholic Church*, 2626 – 2643.

Whom should we pray through?

We should pray through the intercession of the saints. They practiced heroic virtue and lived in fidelity to God's grace so they are proposed to us as models and intercessors. (*CCC* 828). "Being more closely united to Christ, those who dwell in Heaven fix the whole Church more firmly in holiness. They do not cease to intercede with the Father for us, as they proffer the merits which they acquired on earth through the one mediator between God and men, Christ Jesus. So by their fraternal concern is our weakness greatly helped." (*CCC* 956).

We learn from the saints as models of holiness, particularly from the all-holy Virgin Mary, whom the liturgy of the Church celebrates in the rhythms of the Feast Days of the saints. (*CCC* 2030). Mary intercedes for us as she did at Cana when she asked her Son to meet the needs of a wedding feast. (See Jn. 2).

Praying with Our Lady of Guadalupe with the prayers of this book will hopefully be an aid to your personal prayers, reflections and resolutions. You should read the prayers slowly and pause for meditation, application to your own life and make resolutions for your future.

The STORY of
Our Lady of Guadalupe

Our Lady of Guadalupe appeared in Mexico as the pregnant Mother of God to Saint Juan Diego, on December 9, 10 and 12, 1531. She left a Miraculous Image of her appearance on his cactus fiber cloak (tilma), which still exists today for all to see in the Basilica of Our Lady of Guadalupe in Mexico City.

Our Lady came to offer faith, hope and consolation to the oppressed natives of Mexico and to reconcile them with their Spanish rulers. She put an end to the bloody human sacrifice of the Aztecs and converted nine million natives in the next nine years!

The Aztecs practiced human sacrifice as an offering to their false gods. Hernando Cortes and the Spanish conquered and evangelized them.

After the conquest, the Spanish rule of the natives was so severe that a bloody revolt was imminent. Bishop Zumarraga prayed for Our Lady to intervene to prevent an uprising, to reconcile the Spanish and the natives and to bring peace.

On December 9, 1531, Our Lady appeared to Saint Juan Diego who was a recently converted Indian. She asked him to go to the Bishop and request him to build a church for her on the barren hill of Tepeyac which is now part of Mexico City. Our Lady wanted to manifest her Son and show her merciful love to all of her children. The prudent Bishop asked Juan to ask the Lady for a sign. Juan did so and Our Lady promised to give him the sign.

On December 12, Our Lady again appeared to Juan on Tepeyac Hill and told him to pick the Castilian roses which miraculously appeared there and bring them to the Bishop as the sign for him to believe her request. Juan gathered the roses into his tilma and brought them to the Bishop.

He opened the tilma to show them and, to everyone's astonishment, the Image of Our Lady appeared on it. The Bishop then built the church as Our Lady had requested and nine million natives were converted and baptized to the one true faith within the next nine years. Human sacrifice ended in Mexico forever. Our Lady of Guadalupe brought the light of the true faith and established an era of peace.

It has been scientifically established that the Miraculous Image is not a painting. There is no undersizing or pigment in the tilma. It should have rotted after 20 years but it has not decayed after 475 years. In 1921 the tilma survived unscathed from a bomb blast set off directly underneath it by Mexican anti-Catholics.

A digital enhancement of the eyes of the Image show the faces of Saint Juan Diego and Bishop Zumarraga miraculously reflected in the eyes of Our Lady! The distortion and place of the optical reflection in the eyes of Our Lady were identical with what is produced in a human eye. Five eye doctors who examined Our Lady's eye said that they looked into a *human* eye.

Pope Pius XII said that the Miraculous Image was left by "brushes which were not of this earth" and "we are certain that as long as Our Lady of Guadalupe is recognized as Queen and as Mother, America and Mexico will be safe."

Pope John Paul II named Our Lady of Guadalupe as Queen and Mother of America and established December 12 as her Feast Day throughout America. He prayed at her Basilica, "Holy Virgin of Guadalupe, Queen of Peace, save the nations and peoples of this continent!"

The Missionary Image of Our Lady of Guadalupe and Visitations

The Missionary Images are actual (4' x 6') replicas of the original Miraculous Image of Our Lady which she left on Saint Juan Diego's cloak (tilma). They were blessed at the Basilica of Our Lady of Guadalupe in Mexico by the Rector of the Basilica to bring conversions, reverence for life, sanctity of the family and solidarity of the Church in America. They have journeyed on Visitations in the New Evangelization throughout the world. The Images have visited each state of the United States in over one thousand parishes and have received veneration of hundreds of thousands. There have been hundreds of Masses, Confessions, hours of adoration of the Blessed Sacrament and Rosaries in the presence of the Images. Many signs, wonders, conversions, healings, reconciliations and graces are reported.

Many abortions are prevented and at least twenty abortion centers have closed through Our Lady's intercession by her Missionary Image.

The Guardian of the Missionary Images is Dan Lynch of St. Albans, Vermont. He is the Director of a nonprofit tax-exempt apostolate that coordinates the Journey of the Images. He is a retired Judge of the State of Vermont, an author, public speaker and audio and video producer.

Read and see Dan's book, *Our Lady of Guadalupe, Hope for the World* and his video, *Our Lady of Guadalupe, Mother of Hope!,* available from the order form in the back of this book. These explain the history of Our Lady of Guadalupe, her modern mission to end abortion and bring conversions in the New Evangelization through the Missionary Images and the signs, wonders, conversions of their Visitations to churches, abortion centers, monasteries, convents, prisons, hospitals, nursing homes and schools.

Pope John Paul II proclaimed Our Lady of Guadalupe as the Mother of all America. "Now is the time", he said, "of the new evangelization to lead the People of God in America to cross the threshold of the third millennium with renewed hope." He entrusted to her, as the Star of the New Evangelization, the "future path of the Church on the great continent of America."

He looked at an image of Our Lady of Guadalupe and said, "Our Lady is brilliantly seen in the mestizo countenance of this Image of Mary of Guadalupe who appeared at the beginning of the evangelization of the Americas."

"Now Our Lady accompanies each one of her daughters and sons with her motherly presence. I ask her to 'visit' as a 'pilgrim of faith' - each and every diocese, parish and family in America."

The Holy Father said, "May the Continent of Hope also be the Continent of Life! This is our cry: life with dignity for all! The time has come to banish once and for all from the Continent every attack against life. Holy Virgin of Guadalupe, Queen of Peace, save the nations and peoples of this Continent!"

Pope John Paul II's Prophecies for Our Lady of Guadalupe

". . . the sanctuary (of Guadalupe) may become a sort of center from which one may seek a model of Christian spirituality and of familiar converse with God; from which derives an abundance of divine graces and consolations; from which the relations between pastors and faithful, and between all followers of Christ be strengthened; finally from which the light of the Gospel of Christ will shine out over the whole world by means of the miraculous image of His Mother."

(Pope John Paul II, *L'Osservatore Romano*, Vatican City, Jan.25, 1982, p.11).

"In America, the mestiza face of the Virgin of Guadalupe was from the start a symbol of the inculturation of the Gospel, of which she has been the lodestar and the guide. Through her powerful intercession, the Gospel will penetrate the hearts of the men and women of America and permeate their cultures, transforming them from within."

(Pope John II, Apostolic Exhortation, *The Church in America*, No. 70).

Pope John Paul II's Entrustment of the New Evangelization of America to Our Lady of Guadalupe

Pope John Paul II said, "Now is the time of the New Evangelization to lead the People of God in America to cross the threshold of the third millennium with renewed hope." He entrusted to Our Lady of Guadalupe, as the Star of the New Evangelization, the "future path of the Church on the great continent of America." He referred to America in the singular to emphasize the call to all Americans to unity and solidarity.

He said, "From the beginning invoked as 'Our Lady of Guadalupe' Mary, by her motherly and merciful figure, was a great sign of the closeness of the Father and of Jesus Christ, with whom she invites us to enter into communion. . . .

> The appearance of Mary to the native Juan Diego on the hill of Tepeyac in 1531 had a decisive effect on evangelization. Its influence greatly overflows the boundaries of Mexico, spreading to the whole Continent. America, which historically has been, and still is, a melting-pot of peoples, has recognized in the mestiza face of the Virgin of Tepeyac, "in Blessed Mary of Guadalupe, an impressive example of a perfectly inculturated evangelization." Consequently, not only in Central and South America, but in North America as well, the Virgin of Guadalupe is venerated as Queen of all America.
>
> With the passage of time, pastors and faithful alike have grown increasingly conscious of the role of the Virgin Mary in the evangelization of

America. In the prayer composed for the Special Assembly for America of the Synod of Bishops, Holy Mary of Guadalupe is invoked as "Patroness of all America and Star of the first and new evangelization." In view of this, I welcome with joy the proposal of the Synod Fathers that the feast of Our Lady of Guadalupe, Mother and Evangelizer of America, be celebrated throughout the continent on December 12. It is my heartfelt hope that she, whose intercession was responsible for strengthening the faith of the first disciples (cf. Jn 2:11), will by her maternal intercession guide the Church in America, obtaining the outpouring of the Holy Spirit, as she once did for the early Church (cf. Acts 1:14), so that the new evangelization may yield a splendid flowering of Christian life."

(Pope John Paul II, Apostolic Exhortation, *The Church in America*, Nos. 11, 19-24.)

The day after he signed *The Church in America*, Pope John Paul II concelebrated Mass at the Basilica of Our Lady of Guadalupe with hundreds of bishops and priests. He virtually declared the end of the culture of death and preached at the Basilica, "The Church must proclaim the Gospel of Life and speak out with prophetic force against the culture of death. This is our cry: life with dignity for all... The time has come to banish once and for all from the Continent every attack against life... As a matter of urgency, we must stir up a new springtime of holiness on the Continent so that action and contemplation will go hand in hand."

He concluded his homily with a prayer, "Oh, Sweet Lady of Tepeyac, Mother of Guadalupe! We present to you this countless multitude of faithful who pray to God in America. You who have come into their hearts visit and comfort all homes, parishes and dioceses of all the Continent."

Our Lady of Guadalupe and the Gospel of Life

In his Encyclical Letter *The Gospel of Life*, Pope John Paul II referred to the "Great Sign" of the "woman clothed with the sun" from chapter 12 of the Book of Revelation as representing "the mutual relationship between the mystery of the Church and Mary."

This "Woman" is Our Lady of Guadalupe. The "Woman" described in the book of Revelation (See Rev. 12:1-2) is the same as Our Lady of Guadalupe who also appears in her image as a great sign in the sky, a woman clothed with the sun, with the moon under her feet and with child.

Our Lady of Guadalupe appears in her image as a pregnant virgin, signified by the sash tied above her womb and confirmed by gynecological measurements.

The association of Our Lady of Guadalupe with chapter 12 of the Book of Revelation dates from 1648 when the historian Miguel Sanchez first wrote of it. The association was also made in poetry by a seventeenth century nun, Sister Juana Ines de la Cruz, who wrote, "This marvel composed of flowers, Divine American Protectress who from a rose of Castile is transformed into a Mexican rose; she whose proud feet made the Dragon humbly bend his neck…"

Our Lady of Guadalupe is shown in artwork as protecting children from this Red Dragon. (See Rev. 12:4 and the image on page 15). This "American Protectress" is also the Protectress of the Unborn.

She said to Saint Juan Diego, "I will give all my protection to the people. I am the merciful mother of all mankind…. Am I not your fountain of life?" She came to Tepeyac to replace Tonantzin, the false mother goddess that was worshiped there. Our Lady of Guadalupe is a mother who protects her children, both born and unborn, from death.

When Pope John Paul II dedicated a chapel to Our Lady of Guadalupe next to St. Peter's tomb in the Basilica in Rome, he prayed that she would "always defend the gift of life."

Cardinal John O'Connor said, "We commend the Pro-Life Movement of the Archdiocese of New York to the protection and guidance of Our Lady of Guadalupe. . . . Our Lady of Guadalupe pray for America, pray for the unborn."

With the title of *Protectress of the Unborn*, we place under her patronage and protection the Pro-Life Movement and all unborn children. We beg her protection for the mothers of the unborn and the children within their wombs. We ask her to help these mothers to bring their children to birth and to save the souls of those who have been killed by abortions and those who were responsible for them. This has been done on many occasions with the Missionary Image.

In his *Gospel of Life*, Pope John Paul II developed the symbolism of the "Woman" and the "Red Dragon" contained in the Book of Revelation. He said,

> The "Great Sign" of the "Woman" (Rev. 12:1) is accompanied by "another sign which appeared in heaven: a great Red Dragon" (Rev. 12:3), which represents Satan, the personal power of evil, as well as all the powers of evil at work in history and opposing the Church's mission. . . .
>
> Mary thus helps the Church to realize that life is always at the center of a great struggle between good and evil, between light and darkness. The Dragon wishes to devour "the child brought forth" (see Rev. 12:4), a figure of Christ, whom Mary brought forth "in the fullness of time" (Gal. 4:4) and whom the Church must unceasingly offer to people in every age. But in a way that child is also a figure of every person, every child, especially every helpless baby whose life is threatened, be-

cause – as the Council reminds us – "by His Incarnation the Son of God has united Himself in some fashion with every person." It is precisely in the "flesh" of every person that Christ continues to reveal Himself and to enter into fellowship with us, so that rejection of human life, in whatever form that rejection takes, is really a rejection of Christ. This is the fascinating but also demanding truth which Christ reveals to us and which His Church continues untiringly to proclaim: "Whoever receives one such child in my name receives me." (Mt. 18:5); "Truly, I say to you, as you did it to one of the least of these my brethren, you did it to me." (Mt. 25:40).

(Pope John Paul II, Encyclical Letter, *The Gospel of Life*, No. 104).

Opening Prayer for the Mass of Our Lady of Guadalupe

The following is the Opening Prayer for the Mass of the Memorial of Our Lady of Guadalupe celebrated on December 12, the anniversary of her last apparition to Saint Juan Diego, December 12, 1531.

God of power and mercy,
you blessed the Americas at Tepeyac
with the presence of the Virgin Mary of Guadalupe.
May her prayers help all men and women
to accept each other as brothers and sisters.

Through your justice present in our hearts
may your peace reign in the world.
We ask this through our Lord Jesus Christ, your Son,
who lives and reigns with you and the Holy Spirit,
one God, for ever and ever.
Amen.

Words of Our Lady of Guadalupe to Saint Juan Diego and to You

Each of us should read these words as if Our Lady of Guadalupe were speaking to us personally. She graciously identifies herself to us, makes ardent requests, loving promises, gentle admonitions and encourages us to fulfill her requests. We should meditate on how these words apply to us and what our response to her is.

"Know for certain, dearest of my sons, that I am the perfect and perpetual Virgin Mary, Mother of the True God, through whom everything lives, the Lord of all things near and far, the Master of heaven and earth. I ardently desire that a sanctuary be built here for me where I will show Him, I will exalt Him and make Him manifest. I will give Him to the people and offer all my love, my compassion, my help and my protection. I am your merciful Mother, the merciful Mother of all who live united in this land, and of all mankind, of all those who love me, of those who cry to me, of those who have confidence in me. Here I will hear their weeping and their sorrows, and will remedy and alleviate their sufferings, necessities and misfortunes . . . . Be assured that I shall be very grateful and will reward you for doing diligently what I have asked of you. Now that you have heard my words, my son, go and do everything as best as you can."

"Listen to me, my dearest son, and understand that I have many servants and messengers whom I could charge with the delivery of my message. But it is altogether necessary that you should be the one to undertake this mission and that it be through your mediation and assistance that my wish should be accomplished."

"I will wait for you here. Do not forget me."

"What path is this you are taking?"

"Listen and let it penetrate your heart, my dear little son, let nothing discourage you, nothing depress you. Let nothing alter your heart or your countenance. Am I not here who am your Mother? Are you not under my shadow and protection? Am I not your fountain of life? Are you not in the folds of my mantle? In the crossing of my arms? What else do you need? Do not fear any illness or vexation, anxiety or pain."

Pope John Paul II's Prayers

Act of Consecration to Our Lady of Guadalupe

Made by Pope John Paul II during a Mass celebrated in the Basilica of Our Lady of Guadalupe on January 27, 1979. It was his first pilgrimage as Pope and the first time that a pope had visited the Guadalupe Shrine.

O Immaculate Virgin, Mother of the true God and Mother of the Church, who from this place reveal your clemency and your pity to all those who ask for your protection, hear the prayer that we address to you with filial trust, and present it to your Son Jesus, our sole Redeemer.

Mother of Mercy, Teacher of hidden and silent sacrifice, to you, who come to meet us sinners, we dedicate on this day all our being and all our love.

We also dedicate to you our life, our work, our joys, our infirmities and our sorrows.

Grant peace, justice and prosperity to our peoples; for we entrust to your care all that we have and all that we are, Our Lady and Mother.

We wish to be entirely yours and to walk with you along the way of complete faithfulness to Jesus Christ in His Church.

Hold us always with your loving hand.

Virgin of Guadalupe, Mother of the Americas, we pray to you for all the Bishops, that they may lead the faithful along paths of intense Christian life, of love and humble service of God and souls.

Contemplate this immense harvest, and intercede with the Lord that He may instill a hunger for holiness in the whole People of God, and grant abundant vocations of priests and religious, strong in the faith and zealous dispensers of God's mysteries.

Grant to our homes the grace of loving and respecting life in its beginnings, with the same love with which you conceived in your womb the life of the Son of God.

Blessed Virgin Mary, Mother of Fair Love, protect our families, so that they may always be united, and bless the upbringing of our children.

Our hope, look upon us with compassion, teach us to go continually to Jesus and, if we fall, help us to rise again, to return to Him, by means of the confession of our faults and sins in the Sacrament of Penance, which gives peace to the soul.

We beg you to grant us a great love for all the holy Sacraments, which are, as it were, the signs that your Son left us on earth.

Thus, Most Holy Mother, with the peace of God in our conscience, with our hearts free from evil and hatred, we will be able to bring to all true joy and true peace, which come to us from your Son, our Lord Jesus Christ, who with God the Father and the Holy Spirit lives and reigns for ever and ever. Amen.

For a Pilgrimage of Mary in America

Made during an Angelus Address of Pope John Paul II in, Caracas Venezuela, February 11, 1996.

Our Lady accompanies each one of her daughters and sons with her motherly presence. I ask her to "visit" as if on a *peregrinano Mariae* (pilgrimage of Mary), as "a pilgrim of faith" each and every diocese, parish, ecclesial community and family in America, repeating to her children what she said at Cana; "Do whatever he tells you!" (Jn. 2:5). May she cross this continent, bringing it "life, sweetness and hope"! May she enliven and protect the work of the New Evangelization, so that Christians may live their faith with consistency and fervor, and that those who have abandoned it may return. May she promote the unity of the Church, reuniting as in a new Pentecost those who believe in Jesus Christ and those who need to be renewed by the Spirit.

For the Church in America through Our Lady of Guadalupe

Pope John Paul II said, "I invite all the Catholics of America to take an active part in the evangelizing initiatives which the Holy Spirit is stirring in every part of this immense continent, so full of resources and hopes for the future. In a special way, I invite Catholic families to be 'domestic Churches,' in which the Christian faith is lived and passed on to the young as a treasure, and where all pray together. If they live up to the ideal which God places before them, Catholic homes will be true centers of evangelization.

I invite individuals, communities and ecclesial groups, wherever two or more gather in the Lord's name, to strengthen through prayer the spiritual bond between all American Catholics. Let everyone join in the prayer of the Successor of Peter, invoking Christ who is "the way of conversion, communion and solidarity in America."

We thank you, Lord Jesus, because the Gospel of the Father's Love, with which you came to save the world, has been proclaimed far and wide in America as a gift of the Holy Spirit that fills us with gladness.

We thank you for the gift of your Life, which you have given us by loving us to the end: Your Life makes us children of God, brothers and sisters to each other. Increase, O Lord, our faith and our love for you, present in all the tabernacles of the continent.

Grant us to be faithful witnesses to your Resurrection for the younger generation of Americans, so that, in knowing you, they may follow you and find in you their peace and joy.

Only then will they know that they are brothers and sisters of all God's children scattered – throughout the world.

You who, in becoming man, chose to belong to a human family, teach families the virtues which filled with light the family home of Nazareth.

May families always be united, as you and the Father are one, and may they be living witnesses to love, justice and solidarity; make them schools of respect, forgiveness and mutual help, so that the world may believe; help them to be the source of vocations to the priesthood and the consecrated life, and all the other forms of firm Christian commitment.

Protect your Church and the Successor of Peter, to whom you, Good Shepherd, have entrusted the task of feeding your flock. Grant that the Church in America may flourish and grow richer in the fruits of holiness.

Teach us to love your Mother, Mary, as you loved her. Give us the strength to proclaim your word with courage in the work of the New Evangelization, so that the world may know new hope.

Our Lady of Guadalupe, Mother of America, pray for us!

(Pope John Paul II, Apostolic Exhortation, *The Church in America*, No. 76).

For the Sick of America through Our Lady of Guadalupe

Pope John Paul II called Our Lady of Guadalupe "Health of the Sick" and said, "The Church, in her pastoral concern for those who are suffering physically, is close to them with the tenderness and love of Christ. Sickness is a cross, sometimes very heavy, but when united with Christ's Cross it becomes a source of salvation, life and resurrection for the sick person himself and for others. This is why I invite all those who are suffering to offer this trial generously in union with the suffering of Christ and with Mary. Juan Diego heard the Blessed Virgin say: 'Am I not your health;' showing herself as she whom the Christian people always invoke as: 'Salus infirmorum' ('Health of the Sick')."

(*L'Osservatore Romano*, February 11, 1996).

I entrust you all to the Immaculate Virgin, Our Lady of Guadalupe, Patroness of the Americas and Health of the Sick. May she hear the prayers that rise from the world of suffering, may she dry the tears of those in pain, may she stand beside those who are alone in their illness, and by her motherly intercession may she help believers who work in the field of health care to be credible witnesses to Christ's love.

(Pope John Paul II, Eleventh Annual World Day of the Sick Address, February 11, 2003).

Suffering Audrey Santo with the Missionary Image

For Peace through Our Lady of Guadalupe

Made at the end of Pope John Paul II's homily at the Basilica of Our Lady of Guadalupe, Mexico, January 23, 1999.

O Mother! You know the paths followed by the first evangelizers of the New World, from Guanahani Island and Hispaniola to the Amazon forests and the Andean peaks, reaching to Tierra del Fuego in the south and to the Great Lakes and mountains of the north. Accompany the Church which is working in the nations of America, so that she may always preach the Gospel and renew her missionary spirit. Encourage all who devote their lives to the cause of Jesus and the spread of His kingdom.

O gentle Lady of Tepeyac, Mother of Guadalupe! To you we present this countless multitude of the faithful praying to God in America. You who have penetrated their hearts, visit and comfort the homes, parishes and Dioceses of the whole continent. Grant that Christian families may exemplarily raise their children in the Church's faith and in love of the Gospel, so that they will be the seed of apostolic vocations. Turn your gaze today upon young people and encourage them to walk with Jesus Christ.

O Lady and Mother of America! Strengthen the faith of our brothers and sisters, so that in all areas of social, professional, cultural and political life they may act in accord with the truth and the new law which Jesus brought to humanity. Look with mercy on the distress of those suffering from hunger, loneliness, rejection or ignorance. Make us recognize them as your favourite children and give us the fervent charity to help them in their needs.

Holy Virgin of Guadalupe, Queen of Peace! Save the nations and peoples of this continent. Teach everyone, political leaders and citizens, to live in true freedom and to act according to the requirements of justice and respect for human rights, so that peace may thus be established once and for all.

To you, O Lady of Guadalupe, Mother of Jesus and our Mother, belong all the love, honour, glory and endless praise of your American sons and daughters!

For Life to Mary,
Bright Dawn of the New World

Made in Pope John Paul II's Encyclical Letter, The Gospel of Life. *It can be prayed to Our Lady of Guadalupe, since the Pope referred to Our Lady in the prayer as the "Bright Dawn of the New World." This was the role of Our Lady of Guadalupe as the Star of the First Evangelization.*

O Mary
bright dawn of the new world,
Mother of the living,
to you do we entrust the cause of life:
Look down, O Mother,
upon the vast numbers
of babies not allowed to be born,
of the poor whose lives are made difficult,
of men and women
who are victims of brutal violence,
of the elderly and the sick killed
by indifference or out of misguided mercy.
Grant that all who believe in your Son
may proclaim the Gospel of Life
with honesty and love
to the people of our time,
Obtain for them the grace
to accept that Gospel
as a gift ever new,
the joy of celebrating it with gratitude
throughout their lives
and the courage to bear witness to it resolutely,
in order to build,
together with all people of good will,
the civilization of truth and love,
to the praise and glory of God,
the Creator and lover of life.

The Miraculous Image of Our Lady of Guadalupe with light in the form of a fetus over her womb.

For the Families of America through Our Lady of Guadalupe

Pope John Paul II said, "I invite all the Catholics of America to take an active part in the evangelizing initiatives which the Holy Spirit is stirring in every part of this immense continent, so full of resources and hopes for the future. In a special way, I invite Catholic families to be "domestic Churches", in which the Christian faith is lived and passed on to the young as a treasure, and where all pray together. If they live up to the ideal which God places before them, Catholic homes will be true centers of evangelization."

"I invite individuals, communities and ecclesial groups, wherever two or more gather in the Lord's name, to strengthen through prayer the spiritual bond between all American Catholics. Let everyone join in the prayer of the Successor of Peter, invoking Christ who is "the way of conversion, communion and solidarity in America." (Pope John Paul II, Apostolic Exhortation, *The Church in America,* Nos. 294-6.)

Adoptive parents with baby Maria Nicole
and Birth Mom

To St. Juan Diego

Made during Pope John Paul II's homily at the canonization Mass of Saint Juan Diego in the Basilica of Our Lady of Guadalupe, Mexico City, July 31, 2002.

The Pope said, "Beloved brothers and sisters of every ethnic background of Mexico and America, today, in praising the Indian Juan Diego, I want to express to all of you the closeness of the Church and the Pope, embracing you with love and encouraging you to overcome with hope the difficult times you are going through."

Blessed Juan Diego, a good, Christian Indian, whom simple people have always considered a saint! We ask you to accompany the Church on her pilgrimage so that she may be more evangelizing and more missionary each day. Encourage the Bishops, support the priests, inspire new and holy vocations, help all those who give their lives to the cause of Christ and the spread of His Kingdom.

Happy Juan Diego, true and faithful man! We entrust to you our lay brothers and sisters so that, feeling the call to holiness, they may imbue every area of social life with the spirit of the Gospel.

Bless families, strengthen spouses in their marriage, sustain the efforts of parents to give their children a Christian upbringing. Look with favor upon the pain of those who are suffering in body or in spirit, on those afflicted by poverty, loneliness, marginalization or ignorance. May all people, civic leaders and ordinary citizens, always act in accordance with the demands of justice and with respect for the dignity of each person, so that in this way peace may be reinforced.

Beloved Juan Diego, "the Talking Eagle!" Show us the way that leads to the "Dark Virgin" of Tepeyac, that she may receive us in the depths of her heart, for she is the loving, compassionate Mother who guides us to the true God. Amen.

Official canonization image of Saint Juan Diego

Our Lady of Guadalupe requesting St. Juan Diego to go to Bishop Zumarraga.

St. Juan Diego displaying his Tilma to Bishop Zumarraga.

Prayers of Other Popes with Our Lady of Guadalupe

On October 12, 1945, Pope Pius XII re-crowned the Miraculous Image of Our Lady of Guadalupe which was first crowned in 1895 by Pope Leo XII. In his radio address he prayed,

>Hail, Fount most abundant from which springs the streams of Divine Wisdom, repelling with the most pure and limpid waters of othodoxy, the turbulent waves of error. Hail, O Virgin of Guadalupe, Empress of America and Queen of Mexico, we to whom the admirable ordering of Divine Providence has confided – without taking into consideration our unworthiness – the sacred treasure of Divine Wisdom on earth, for the salvation of all souls, place again today above your brow the crown, which puts forever under your powerful patronage the purity and the integrity of the holy faith in Mexico and in all the American continents.
>
>For we are certain that as long as you are recognized as Queen and as Mother, the Americas and Mexico will be safe.

On October 12, 1961, Pope John XXIII gave a radio address on the occasion of the solemn closing of a year dedicated to Our Lady of Guadalupe. He prayed,

>Hail Mother of the Americas, Heavenly Missionary of the New World! From the Sanctuary of Tepeyac you have been for more than four centuries the Mother and Teacher of the Faith to the peoples of the Americas. Be also our protection and save us, O Immaculate Mary. Aid our rulers. Stir up a new zeal in our prelates. Increase the virtues of our clergy, and preserve forever our Faith.

In every home may the holiness of the family flourish, and in the shelter of the home may Catholic education, favored by your own benign glance, achieve a wholesome growth. Amen.

On November 20, 1962, in Our Lady of Guadalupe Church, Rome, Pope John XXIII prayed,

Our Lady of Guadalupe, you who have desired to give special signs of benevolence to the land of Mexico and have promised consolation and help to those who love you and follow you, gaze kindly on all of your children. They invoke you with confidence.

Preserve in our souls the precious gift of divine grace. Make us docile to the will of Our Lord in such a manner that His reign may be extended more and more in our hearts, in our families and in our beloved nation.

O most holy Virgin, be with us in the fatigues of our daily work, in the joys as well as in the pains and difficulties of life, so that our immortal spirit may rise, free and pure, to God, and that we may serve Him joyfully with generosity and fervor.

Defend us from all evil, O Queen and Mother of Mexico, and make us faithful imitators of your Divine Son, Jesus, who is the Way, the Truth, and the Life, so that one day, guided by your hand, we may reach the reward of the beatific vision in heaven. Amen.

Meditations with Our Lady of Guadalupe on the Mysteries of the Rosary

The Joyful Mysteries

The Annunciation

The angel Gabriel announced to the Virgin Mary that she would be a mother and would conceive and bear a son who would be called "Son of the Most High." (Lk. 1:32). She accepted her pregnancy and said, "I am the servant of the Lord. Let it be done to me as you say." (Lk. 1:38).

Our Lady of Guadalupe announced to St. Juan Diego that she was, "The perfect and perpetual Virgin Mary, Mother of the one true God through whom we live."

Let us pray that all will come to know, believe, trust and love the one true God and that all mothers will accept their pregnancies with the humble and trustful attitude of Mary.

The Visitation

After the Annunciation, Mary went in haste to visit her elderly pregnant cousin Elizabeth who said, "Blest is she who trusted that the Lord's words would be fulfilled." (Lk. 1:45).

After the Annunciation of Our Lady of Guadalupe, St. Juan Diego trusted that her words would be fulfilled. He went to visit Bishop Zumarraga to convey her request that he build a church so that she could manifest her Son to the people.

Let us pray that all will come to trust the Word of the Lord and to care for pregnant mothers, as did Mary for Elizabeth.

The Nativity

On the first Christmas, Mary manifested her newborn son at Bethlehem to shepherds and they adored Him. (Lk. 2:16).

On the day after Christmas in 1531, Our Lady of Guadalupe manifested her Son to the Spanish and the Indians in the new church built by Bishop

Zumarraga in Mexico at Tepeyac Hill and they adored Him.

Let us pray that all will come to adore Jesus Christ as the Son of Man and the Son of God and will welcome all newborn children.

The Presentation

Mary presented her Son in the Temple and Simeon said, "This child is destined to be the downfall and the rise of many in Israel . . . . " (Lk. 2:34).

Our Lady of Guadalupe presented her Son in the church on Tepeyac Hill and began the rising of millions in Mexico to the one true faith of the Catholic Church.

Let us pray that all will come to know and believe in the one true faith of the Catholic Church and present their children to God in thanksgiving for His gift of them.

The Finding in the Temple

Joseph and Mary found their twelve-year-old son teaching in the Temple. (Lk. 2:46). They were re-united as a family and He was obedient to them. (Lk. 2:51).

Mary's son, St. Juan Diego, was found teaching in the church on Tepeyac where he stayed for the last fourteen years of his life explaining the apparitions and the messages of Our Lady of Guadalupe.

Let us pray that all will accept the teachings of the Catholic Church and for the reunions of all divided families and the obedience of children to their parents.

The Luminous Mysteries

Christ's Baptism in the Jordan

John the Baptist baptized Jesus in the River Jordan. (Mt. 3:13). Jesus came out of the water and a voice from the heavens said, "This is my beloved Son." (Mt 3:17).

After the apparitions of Our Lady of Guadalupe, nine million Indians were baptized within the next nine years in the greatest mass evangelization in the history of the world. Baptism makes us adopted children of God.

Let us pray for a New Evangelization in which all come to Baptism and the realization that we are all children of God, particularly the unborn and all marginalized people.

Christ's Self-Manifestation at the Wedding of Cana

Jesus manifested Himself by His first public miracle by changing water into wine at the Wedding of Cana through the intercession of Mary. He revealed His glory and His disciples believed in Him. (Jn. 2:11).

Our Lady of Guadalupe manifested Jesus through her intercession in the first public miracle in Mexico by leaving her pregnant image on St. Juan Diego's tilma (cloak) at his audience with Bishop Zumarraga. The Bishop believed in her.

Let us pray that all come to believe in Jesus as Son of the one true God and Our Lady of Guadalupe as Mother of the one true God, as she identified herself to St. Juan Diego. Let us pray for strong Christian marriages united in love with an openness to new life.

Christ's Proclamation of the Kingdom

Jesus said, "This is the time of fulfillment. The kingdom of God is at hand. Reform your lives and believe in the Gospel." (Mk. 1:15). "I tell you, that is why her many sins are forgiven - because of her great love. Little is forgiven the one whose love is small." (Lk. 7:47).

Our Lady of Guadalupe desired to reveal the kingdom

of God, the Gospel and the forgiveness of sins. She told St. Juan Diego, "I want to manifest Him to the people."

Let us pray that all will reform their lives, believe in the Gospel, receive the forgiveness of their sins and come into the kingdom of God. Let us pray particularly for those who have committed or supported the following sins against life: contraception, sterilization, abortion, homosexuality, in vitro fertilization, embryonic experimentation and cloning.

Christ's Transfiguration

On the mountain, Jesus transfigured His appearance into dazzling white. The Father spoke from a cloud and said, "This is my Son, my Chosen One. Listen to Him." (Lk. 9:35).

On Tepeyac Mountain, Mary appeared in dazzling white to St. Juan Diego and said, "I am the Mother of the one true God."

Let us pray that all adore Jesus really present in the Eucharist and listen to Him when He speaks to us in our hearts, through the Gospel and through the Church.

Christ's Institution of the Eucharist

Jesus took bread, gave thanks, broke it and gave it to His apostles, saying, "This is my body to be given for you . . . . This cup is the new covenant in my blood, which will be shed for you." (Lk. 22:19-20).

Our Lady of Guadalupe desired to reveal her Son in the Eucharist and requested St. Juan Diego to ask Bishop Zumarraga to build a church where she could "manifest Him to the people."

Let us pray that all come to recognize the real presence of Jesus in the Eucharist.

The Sorrowful Mysteries

The Agony in the Garden

Jesus agonized in the Garden of Gethsemane over His impending passion and death. He said, "My heart is nearly broken with sorrow." (Mt. 26:38). He asked His apostles to stay awake with Him and pray. But they fell asleep.

Our Lady of Guadalupe agonized from heaven over the impending passion and deaths by human sacrifice of 20% of the Indian children each year in 16th century Mexico. What they did to them they did to Jesus who said, "As you did it to one of the least of these my brethren, you did it to me." (Mt. 25:40).

Let us pray that we stay awake with Jesus and Mary and pray with them to relieve the agony of their sorrow over the impending deaths by human sacrifice by abortion of 25% of the unborn children in the United States each year.

The Scourging at the Pillar

Pontius Pilate had Jesus scourged by flailing His body with whips that ripped His skin and exposed His bones. (Mt. 27:26).

Our Lady of Guadlaupe watched with sorrow from heaven as the Aztec priests ripped open the chests of the victims of their human sacrifices and tore out their beating hearts that they offered to their false idols.

Let us pray with Jesus and Mary against our Culture of Death that legalizes human sacrifice by abortion which rips and kills the beating hearts of unborn children. Let us pray for a Culture of Life and a civilization of love.

The Crowning of Thorns

Pilate's soldiers weaved a crown out of thorns and they fixed it on Jesus' head, spat at Him and mocked Him. (Mt. 27:29).

Our Lady of Guadalupe looked on with sorrow from heaven as the Aztecs mocked God's plan for human life and sexuality by their practice of homosexuality.

Let us pray with Jesus and Mary against legalized sodomy and homosexual unions. Let us pray for indissoluble monogamous marriages. of one man and one woman who practice human sexuality by uniting in love with an openness to new life.

The Carrying of the Cross

"They took Jesus and led Him away. And carrying the Cross for Himself, He went forth to the place called the Skull, in Hebrew, Golgotha." (Jn. 19:16-17).

Our Lady of Guadalupe looked on with sorrow from heaven as the Aztecs led their victims to their Golgothas, the temples of human sacrifice.

Let us pray with Jesus and Mary that all mothers carry their unborn children to life and not to abortion centers that are the Golgothas of the modern world.

The Crucifixion

Jesus was crucified and died on the Cross. As He was dying He said from His Cross to the disciple whom He loved, "Behold your Mother." (Jn. 19:27).

Our Lady of Guadalupe told St. Juan Diego, "I am your merciful Mother." He cared for his dying elderly uncle, Juan Bernardino. As he lay dying on his bed, he beheld his mother, Our Lady of Guadalupe, who appeared to him and healed him.

Let us pray with Jesus and Mary that all of the sick and dying are cared for and not deliberately killed and that all behold Our Lady of Guadalupe as our merciful mother.

The Glorious Mysteries

The Resurrection

On Easter Sunday morning, Mary Magdalene came to the tomb of Jesus. Suddenly an angel descended from heaven and told her, "Do not be frightened. I know you are looking for Jesus the crucified, but He is not here. He has been raised, exactly as He promised. (Mt. 28:5-6).

On the day after Christmas in 1531, the miraculous image of Our Lady of Guadalupe was processed to Tepeyac Hill. In jubilation, the Indians shot their arrows into the air. An Indian was accidentally killed by one of the arrows. He was brought beneath the miraculous image and raised from the dead through the intercession of Our Lady of Guadalupe. This was symbolic of the raising of the Aztec Culture of Death to a new Culture of Life.

Let us pray that our Culture of Death be raised to a new Culture of Life through the intercession of Our Lady of Guadalupe.

The Ascension

After the apparitions of the risen Christ, He told his apostles, "Go into the whole world and proclaim the Good News to all creation. The man who believes in it and accepts Baptism will be saved. . . . Then, after speaking to them, the Lord Jesus, was taken up into heaven and took His seat at God's right hand." (Mk. 16:15-16, 19).

After the apparitions of Our Lady of Guadalupe, missionary priests proclaimed the Good News to the Indians in the First Evangelization in America. Nine million were baptized within the next nine years.

Let us pray that millions believe in the Good News and accept Baptism in a New Evangelization in America through the intercession of Our Lady of Guadalupe.

The Descent of the Holy Spirit

At the first Pentecost, the Holy Spirit descended upon and filled the apostles. Peter preached to the Jews staying in Jerusalem from every nation under heaven. He said, " 'You must reform and be baptized each one of you, in the name of Jesus Christ, that your sins may be forgiven; then you will receive the gift of the Holy Spirit.' . . . Some three thousand were baptized that day." (Acts 3: 38; 41).

After the apparitions of Our Lady of Guadalupe, millions of Indians reformed and were baptized in the name of Jesus Christ and received the forgiveness of their sins and the Holy Spirit. An average of three thousand Indians were baptized each day over a period of nine years for a total of nine million Baptisms in a novena of nine years of daily Pentecosts.

Let us pray that millions will answer Peter's call to reform and be baptized in the name of Jesus Christ with millions of Baptisms in a New Pentecost.

The Assumption

Soon after her life on earth, Mary's body and soul were assumed into heavenly glory. (Vatican II, *Dogmatic Constitution on the Church*, No. 59). "A great sign appeared in the sky, a woman clothed with the sun, with the moon under her feet, and on her head a crown of twelve stars. She was with child." (Rev. 12:1-2). "Then another sign appeared in the sky. It was a huge red dragon that stood before the woman about to give birth, ready to devour her child." (Rev 12:3-4).

The miraculous image of the pregnant Lady of Guadalupe is this image described in chapter twelve of the Book of Revelation. The red dragon represents Satan who seeks to devour all unborn children. Our Lady of Guadalupe's intercession ended the human sacrifice of the children of Mexico.

Let us pray that all recognize the great sign of Our Lady of Guadalupe and pray with her for the end of the modern human sacrifice by abortion of unborn children. Let us respect pregnant mothers and help them to bring their children to birth.

The Coronation

After Our Lady's Assumption into heaven, the Lord exalted her as Queen over all things. Jesus crowned His Mother as Queen of heaven and earth and of all the angels and saints. As our charitable Mother, she continues to care for us on earth who journey toward our heavenly home surrounded by dangers and difficulties under her safe guidance and protection. (Vatican II, *Dogmatic Constitution on the Church*, No. 62).

Pope Pius XII ordered that the miraculous image of Our Lady of Guadalupe be crowned. He said, "We are certain that as long as you are recognized as Queen and Mother, Mexico and the Americas will be safe." Pope John Paul II prayed to her, "Since you are the Empress of the Americas, protect all the nations of the American continents and the ones that brought faith and love for you there."

Let us pray that all recognize Our Lady of Guadalupe as our Queen and Mother and let us pray for her protection and the safety of all of the nations of the Americas.

Novena to Our Lady of Guadalupe

PATRONESS OF ALL AMERICA
PRAY FOR US

U.S. Bishops' Novena to Our Lady of Guadalupe, Patroness of All America

This is the National Conference of Catholic Bishops' Novena. It may be prayed during any nine-day period, and is most appropriate in the nine days preceeding the feast of Our Lady of Guadalupe on December 12.

ON THE FIRST DAY
Mary, Mother of Jesus, hear the prayer of the Church in America, a people rich in promise, a people much in need of God's mercy. As you first brought faith to these lands, be with us in the third millinnium of our redemption.
REFRAIN
O Lady of Guadalupe, pray for the Church in America and walk with us in the third millennium of faith.
Our Father . . . , Hail Mary . . . (3x), Glory be . . .

ON THE SECOND DAY
Mary, Mother of America, hear the many voices of our land, pleading for the mercy of your Son, seeking the shepherd's voice to lead them home. Hear the praise of your sons and daughters and bid your Son to free us from the scourges of addiction, selfishness and want.
REFRAIN O Lady of Guadalupe . . .
Our Father . . . , Hail Mary . . . (3x), Glory be . . .

ON THE THIRD DAY
Mary, Mother of Compassion, hear the prayer of those most in need of God's mercy. Hear the little child whose belly hungers, the old man with no one to love, the mother tempted to abandon her child. Pray for them to the author of life, that the fruit of your womb may save and protect them.
REFRAIN O Lady of Guadalupe . . .
Our Father . . . , Hail Mary . . . (3x), Glory be . . .

ON THE FOURTH DAY
Mary, Mother of Conversion, pray to your Son for the virtue of hope. Pray Him to free us from doubt and to give us the courage of the children of God. Pray that the light of the world may dispel the darkness of our fear, remaking our stony hearts in the image of the Sacred Heart of Jesus your Son.
REFRAIN O Lady of Guadalupe . . .
Our Father . . . , Hail Mary . . . (3x), Glory be . . .

ON THE FIFTH DAY
   Mary, Mother of all Saints, pray for your children in America. Pray for those who seek to imitate your example in humble service to the Gospel of Life and the poorest of the poor. Pray that your Son may lead us from the darkness of sin to the light of His eternal glory.
REFRAIN O Lady of Guadalupe . . .
Our Father . . . , Hail Mary . . . (3x), Glory be . . .

ON THE SIXTH DAY
   Mary, Mother of Unity, intercede for the Church in America, that we may be gathered together to form the one people of the New Covenant. Mother of the human race, ask your Son to pour out upon us a spirit of compassion and solidarity.
REFRAIN O Lady of Guadalupe . . .
Our Father . . . , Hail Mary . . . (3x), Glory be . . .

ON THE SEVENTH DAY
   Mary, Mother of the Church, help the Church in these lands to follow your example of sublime love and profound humility. With you, may we be obedient to the commandment of love, and give ourselves wholeheartedly to seeking the glory of Christ and serving the needs of our brothers and sisters.
REFRAIN O Lady of Guadalupe . . .
Our Father . . . , Hail Mary . . . (3x), Glory be . . .

ON THE EIGHTH DAY
   Mary, Mother of all Christians, hear the prayers of all who worship the name of your Son, Jesus, our hope and salvation. Under the protection of your prayers, may the Church in America enjoy unbroken peace.
REFRAIN O Lady of Guadalupe . . .
Our Father . . . , Hail Mary . . . (3x), Glory be . . .

ON THE NINTH DAY
   God of power and mercy, you blessed the Americas at Tepeyac with the presence of the Virgin Mary of Guadalupe. By her prayers enable all people to accept each other as brothers and sisiters. Instill justice in our hearts that your peace may reign in the world. We ask this through our Lord Jesus Christ, your Son, who lives and reigns with you in the unity of the Holy Spirit, God forever and ever.
REFRAIN O Lady of Guadalupe . . .
Our Father . . . , Hail Mary . . . (3x), Glory be . . .

The Way of the Cross with Our Lady of Guadalupe

The Passion of the Christ
for
The Unborn Victims

Introduction

The Meaning of Christ's Passion

The Passion of Christ didn't just happen by chance. It is part of the mystery of God's plan, as St. Peter explains in his first sermon on Pentecost, "This Jesus [was] delivered up according to the definite plan and foreknowledge of God." (Acts 2:23).

But this doesn't mean that those who caused Christ's Passion were just puppets carrying out God's plan on His strings. They were free to do what they did and God permitted it. *The Catechism of The Catholic Church* (*CCC*) teaches, "To God, all moments of time are present in their immediacy. When therefore He establishes His eternal plan of "predestination," He includes in it each person's free response to His grace." (*CCC* 600). So, for the sake of accomplishing His plan of salvation, God permitted the acts that flowed from the blindness of Pontius Pilate, King Herod, the soldiers and the crowd. But it wasn't just them that caused Christ's Passion.

The Church teaches that sinners in the past, as well as sinners today, caused the Passion of Christ. "We must regard as guilty all those who continue to relapse into their sins. Since our sins made the Lord Christ suffer the torment of the Cross, those who plunge themselves into disorders and crimes crucify the Son of God anew in their hearts (for He is in them) and hold Him up to contempt." (*CCC* 598).

The prophet Isaiah foretold God's divine plan of salvation through the putting to death of "the righteous one, my Servant" as a mystery that would free all humanity from the slavery of sin. (Is. 53). "Jesus' redemptive death fulfills Isaiah's prophecy of the suffering Servant." (*CCC* 601).

John the Baptist looked at Jesus when he baptized Him and pointed Him out as the "Lamb of God, who takes away the sin of the world." (Jn. 1:29). "By doing so, he reveals that Jesus is at the same time the suffering Servant who silently allows Himself to be led to the slaughter and who bears the sin of the multitudes, and also the Paschal Lamb, the symbol of Israel's redemption at the first Passover. Christ's whole life expresses His mission: "to serve and to give His life as a ransom for many." (Mk. 10:45; *CCC* 608).

"By embracing in His human heart the Father's love for men, Jesus "loved them to the end," for "greater love has no man than this, that a man lay down His life for His friends." (Jn. 15:13) . . . Jesus freely accepted His Passion and death: "No one takes [my life] from me, but I lay it down of my own accord." (Jn. 10:18). Hence the sovereign freedom of God's Son as He went out to His death." (*CCC* 609).

Jesus accomplished the substitution of the suffering Servant of Isaiah, who "makes himself an offering for sin," when "He bore the sin of many," and who "shall make many to be accounted righteous," for "He shall bear their iniquities." (Is. 53:10-12; *CCC* 615).

"It is love 'to the end' that confers on Christ's sacrifice its value as redemption and reparation, as atonement and satisfaction. He knew and loved us all when He offered His life. . . . No man, not even the holiest, was ever able to take on himself the sins of all men and offer himself as a sacrifice for all. The existence in Christ of the divine person of the Son, who at once surpasses and embraces all human persons and constitutes Himself as the head of all mankind, makes possible His redemptive sacrifice for all." (*CCC* 616).

Why We Should Meditate on Christ's Passion

We should do more than just think about Christ's Passion, we should actively meditate on it, envisioning it in our imagination, helped by the images and words of the event. We should meditate on the Passion as shown on the Way of the Cross because it is the greatest love story ever told.

God is love. (Jn. 4:8). Out of love for us He emptied Himself of glory. (Phil. 2:6-11). The Word was made flesh and He became one of us. (Jn. 1:13). It was not God's perfect will that Jesus should die at our hands. Rather, He permitted it and Jesus entrusted Himself to us, our free will, and ultimately into our hands and sins that killed Him. As Isaiah prophesied, it was our hands that killed Him. (Is. 53). Jesus died so that we might live in eternal life with Him through the forgiveness of our sins merited by His Passion and death.

Jesus said, "Greater love has no man than this, that a man lay down His life for His friends." (Jn. 15:13). We are His friends and He showed us this greater love by laying down His life through His Passion and death. He loved us and forgave us to the end and said, "Father forgive them, for they know not what they do." (Lk. 23:34).

The greatest virtues of love are humility and obedience because it was the opposite vices, pride and disobedience, that caused the Original Sin of Adam and Eve. Jesus is the New Adam whose virtues of humility and obedience repaired for the vices of pride and disobedience of Adam and Eve.

"Christ Jesus . . . humbled Himself and became obedient unto death, even death on a Cross. Therefore, God has highly exalted Him." (Phil. 2:6,8-9). This wonderful hymn of the Letter of St.

Paul to the Philippians reminds us that because of Christ's Passion and death God exalted Him through the glory of His Resurrection.

When we meditate on Christ's Passion, we see the best examples of the exercise of every virtue. Christ displays humility, obedience, patience, charity, meekness and unshaken firmness of soul. Christ in His Passion is our model of holiness to be imitated by us.

Christ's Passion is our Model for Holiness

In the First Letter of Peter, he tells us that Christ is our model of holiness and the example that we are to follow, walking in His very footsteps. Jesus said, "If any man would come after me, let him deny himself and take up his cross and follow me." (Mk. 8:34).

St. Peter says,

> For to this you have been called, because Christ also suffered for you, leaving you an example, that you should follow in His steps. He committed no sin; no guile was found on His lips. When He was reviled, He did not revile in return; when He suffered, He did not threaten; but He trusted to Him who judges justly. He Himself bore our sins in His body on the tree, that we might die to sin and live to righteousness. By His wounds you have been healed. For you were straying like sheep, but have now returned to the Shepherd and Guardian of your souls. (1 Pt. 21-24).

The Way of the Cross

We can "follow in His steps," as St. Peter urged us, by praying the Way of the Cross, also known as the Stations of the Cross. There are 14 Stations of the Cross. They are based on Scripture and oral tradition. The scriptural Stations are 1, 2, 5 and 8. (Jn. Ch.19). These Stations are located in Jerusalem. They are the places at which Jesus suffered on the way to Calvary from the place of His condemnation by Pontius Pilate to His crucifixion on Calvary and His burial in the nearby tomb. These Stations are a very short distance on the ground in the city of Jerusalem, probably no more than a quarter of a mile. The tradition is that the Antonia fortress and the Praetorium nearby were the sites where Jesus was brought before Pilate.

The fortress, which stood near the north-west corner of the Jewish Temple, was the beginning of the way of the walk of Jesus carrying His Cross.

He carried it to Mount Calvary that was then located outside the city walls. Today, Stations 1 through 9 are located in the streets of Jerusalem and Stations 10 through 14 are located inside the Church of the Holy Sepulchre.

The Way of the Cross was first prayed by His Mother but they only came into popular use on the streets of Jerusalem in the 16th century. The Stations are often represented by plaques or paintings along the interior walls of Catholic churches. The Stations are prayed by visiting them in the churches with or without a leader or by praying them outside of churches with the images in this booklet and meditating on Christ's Passion suffered for us. This devotion is encouraged by the Church, especially on Fridays and during Lent.

The Way of the Cross is prayed at the Stations on the walls of churches by proceeding from Station to Station if able or, if not, proceeding on the Way in our imagination. This is a devotion by which we believe, adore, trust and love Jesus for suffering His Passion for us. We make pilgrimages in spirit to the principle scenes of Christ's suffering and death.

We should meditate on each Station just as if we were really there with Jesus in Jerusalem. We should place ourselves in the scene as if we were Jesus and imagine how He felt physically, emotionally and spiritually with His pain and suffering. Then we engage in conversation with Him about the Station.

We should remember that Jesus said, "So, could you not watch with me one hour?" (Mt. 26:40). So, we should pray slowly and meditatively and we should expect to take about an hour to accompany Jesus on His Way. We should not rush on the Way of the Cross.

The Way of the Cross
with
Our Lady of Guadalupe for the Unborn Victims

Abortion and embryonic killing are horrible evils because they are a direct attack against God, the Author of human life. They are a direct attack by Satan against innocence and against motherhood. Therefore, they are a direct attack against Jesus and His holy Mother, Mary, in the great struggle for life. They are re-Crucifixions of the innocent helpless Christ who said, "Truly, I say to you, as you did it to one of the least of these my brethren, you did it to me." (Mt. 25:40). The least of His brethren are the innocent unborn children.

The unborn children who are aborted and the embryos who are killed are martyrs for the truth that human life begins and is endowed with inviolable dignity at conception. So too were the Holy Innocents martyrs for the truth that Jesus was the true king of Israel. "Blessed are those who are persecuted for righteousness sake, for theirs is the kingdom of heaven." (Mt. 5:10).

Our Lady of Guadalupe is our intercessor for life because she is at the center of the struggle for life. She appeared in Mexico as the pregnant Mother of God to Saint Juan Diego, a Chicemeca Indian, on December 9, 10 and 12, 1531. She left a Miraculous Image of her appearance on his cactus fiber cloak, or "tilma," which still exists today for all to see in the Basilica of Our Lady of Guadalupe in Mexico City.

Our Lady of Guadalupe put an end to the bloody human sacrifice of the Aztec Indians and converted nine million natives in the next nine years. We pray through her intercession that she will end the modern human sacrifices of abortion and embryonic killing and convert millions in the New Evangelization.

When Pope John Paul II came to the Basilica of Our Lady of Guadalupe in January of 1999, he preached in his homily, "The

Church must proclaim the Gospel of Life and speak out with prophetic force against the Culture of Death. This is our cry: life with dignity for all. . . . The time has come to banish once and for all from the Continent every attack against life."

God wants those guilty of abortion and embryonic killings to be reconciled to Him and those killed to be saved. This will be accomplished through the blood shed by the innocents and our reparatory prayer, sacrifice, sacramental receptions and desire for their salvation through the intercession of Our Lady of Guadalupe.

Jesus in His incarnate divine person has mysteriously united Himself to every human being, including the unborn children. He calls us to take up our cross and follow in His steps. This is what his Mother did and so should we. (*CCC* 618).

So, we spiritually accompany Him and His Mother on the Way of the Cross. Since Mary was present at the crucifixion according to Scripture (see Jn. 19), she probably was present at all of the Stations. It is unlikely that she would be at the end, if she were not there from the beginning. So, in the meditations for these Stations, Mary, under the title of Our Lady of Guadalupe, is spiritually present with the killed unborn children seen in Jesus. Our Lady of Guadalupe stands in support of the innocence of unborn children and intercedes for their lives and the salvation of them and their parents and killers. These are the ones for whom we pray. They are the victims of the Culture of Death. We also pray through the intercession of Blessed Mother Teresa and Servant of God Dorothy Day.

Blessed Mother Teresa meditated often on the Passion of the Christ. She said, "For my meditation I am using the Passion of Jesus. I am afraid I make no meditation but only look at Jesus suffer and keep repeating, 'Let me share with you His pain!' " She also said that abortion was the greatest destroyer of peace and that what we do to the unborn child, we do to Jesus.

In her Nobel Prize Acceptance Speech she said,

> I feel the greatest destroyer of peace today is abortion, because it is a direct war, a direct killing, direct murder by the mother herself. And we read in the scripture, for God says very clearly: "Even if a mother could forget her child, I will not forget you. I have carved you in the palm of my hand." We are carved in the palm of His hand; so close to Him, that unborn child has been carved in the hand of God. . . .
>
> Millions are dying deliberately by the will of the mother. And this is what is the greatest destroyer of peace today. Because if a mother can kill her own child, what is left but for me to kill you and you to kill me? There is nothing between. . . .
>
> And this is why we believe what Jesus has said: "I was hungry; I was naked, I was homeless; I was unwanted, unloved, uncared for — and you did it to me."

Mother Teresa also told President Clinton and other American leaders at the National Prayer Breakfast, "If we remember that God loves us, and that we can love others as He loves us, then America can become a sign of peace for the world. From here, a sign of care for the weakest of the weak — the unborn child — must go out to the world."

Dorothy Day once said, "The Sexual Revolution is a complete rebellion against authority, natural and supernatural, even against the body and its needs, its natural functions of child bearing. This is not reverence for life, it is a great denial and more resembles Nihilism than the revolution that they think they are furthering."

Dorothy lived her own sexual revolution when she was young. She had an abortion that she always regretted and later converted to the Catholic church. Cardinal John O'Connor introduced her cause for canonization and she is now a Servant of God. He said, "I wish every woman who has ever suffered an abortion would come to know Dorothy Day. Her story was so typical. Made pregnant by a man who insisted she have an abortion, who then abandoned her anyway, she suffered terribly for what she had done, and later pleaded with others not to do the same."

"But later, too, after becoming a Catholic, she learned the love and mercy of the Lord, and knew she never had to worry about His forgiveness. (This is why I have never condemned a woman who has had an abortion; I weep with her and ask her to remember Dorothy Day's sorrow but to know always God's loving mercy and forgiveness.)"

Plenary Indulgence

The Church grants a plenary indulgence to those who make the Way of the Cross, at the Stations of the Cross, in a Catholic church, in the manner described in this booklet. A plenary indulgence remits the temporal punishment due to our sins that have been forgiven in the sacrament of Confession but for which just punishment remains either in this world or in Purgatory. This punishment is forgiven under the usual conditions of release from attachment to sin and attendance at Mass, reception of Holy Communion and prayers for the Holy Father's intentions within eight days of praying the Stations.

Manner

The Way of the Cross is done in this manner:

The Leader reads the name of the Station, at each Station, and moves from one Station to the next.

All sing the verse for the Station to the melody of the Spiritual, *Were You There When They Crucified My Lord?*

The Leader prays, "We adore you, O Christ, and we praise you."

All respond, "Because by your Holy Cross, you have redeemed the world."

Jesus speaks to us through the Leader who reads the excerpt from The Reproaches from the Veneration of the Cross from the Liturgy of the Lord's Passion (Good Friday) and the scriptural passage for the Station. All meditate on these.

All speak to Jesus and read a conversation addressed to Him reflecting on the Station and His representation today of killed unborn children.

All pray the Concluding Prayers. Imploring God's mercy from the Chaplet of Divine Mercy that was revealed to Saint Faustina.

All sing a stanza to the melody of the *Stabat Mater* (The Standing Mother). This reminds us of Mary's standing at the Station. The stanzas were composed by the author.

If there is no leader, read and pray all of the parts.

Pope John Paul II said, "A great prayer for life is urgently needed, a prayer which will rise up throughout the world. (Pope John Paul II, Encyclical Letter, *The Gospel of Life*). The prayers of this booklet can help to answer the call of the Holy Father.

Preface and Opening Scripture

Leader: At the beginning of the *Way of the Cross* on Good Friday 2000, Pope John Paul II said, "We are here because we are convinced that the *Way of the Cross* of the Son of God was not simply a journey to the place of execution. We believe that every step of the condemned Christ, every action and every word, as well as everything felt and done by those who took part in this tragic drama, continues to speak to us. In His suffering and death too, Christ reveals to us the truth about God and man."

A Reading from The Book of The Prophet Isaiah.

He was despised and rejected by men; a man of sorrows, and acquainted with grief; and as one from whom men hide their faces he was despised, and we esteemed him not.

Surely he has borne our grief and carried our sorrows; yet we esteemed him stricken, smitten by God, and afflicted. But he was wounded for our transgressions, he was bruised for our iniquities; upon him was the chastisement that made us whole, and with his stripes we are healed. All we like sheep have gone astray; we have turned every one to his own way; and the LORD has laid on him the iniquity of us all.

He was oppressed, and he was afflicted, yet he opened not his mouth; like a lamb that is led to the slaughter, and like a sheep that before its shearers is dumb, so he opened not his mouth. By oppression and judgment he was taken away; and as for his generation, who considered that he was cut off out of the land of the living, stricken for the transgression of my people? And they made his grave with the wicked and with a rich man in his death, although he had done no violence, and there was no deceit in his mouth. (Is. 53:3-9).

The Word of the Lord.

All: Thanks be to God.

Opening Prayer

Leader: Pope John Paul II addressed the congregation on Good Friday 2004 before The *Way of the Cross* at the Roman Coliseum. He said,

All: We follow Christ's Way of the Cross and participate in that "hour" in which the Redemption was fulfilled. The hour "to depart out of this world to the Father." (Jn. 13:1). The hour of the heart-rending suffering of the Son of God, a suffering that, 20 centuries later, continues to overwhelm and question us profoundly.

The Son of God came to this hour (see Jn. 12:27) precisely to give His life for His brothers. It is the "hour" to hand Himself over, the "hour" of the revelation of infinite love.

"The hour has come for the Son of man to be glorified." (Jn. 12:23). This is the "hour" in which we, men and women of all times, have been given the love that is stronger than death. We are beneath the Cross on which the Son of God is nailed so that with the power that the Father has given Him over all human beings He may give eternal life to all those who have been given to Him. (See Jn. 17:2).

Is it not, therefore, a duty in this "hour" to give glory to God the Father "who did not spare His own Son but gave Him up for us all?" (Rom. 8:32).

Has not the moment come to glorify the Son who "humbled Himself and became obedient unto death, even death on a Cross?" (Phil. 2:8).

How is it possible not to give glory to the Spirit of Him who resurrected Christ from the dead and who now dwells in us to also give life to our mortal bodies? (See Rom. 8:11).

May this "hour" of the Son of man remain in our minds and hearts as the "hour of love and of glory."

May the mystery of the Way of the Cross of the Son of God be for all an inexhaustible source of hope. May it console and strengthen us also when our hour comes.

Leader: Jesus prophesied, "Behold, we are going up to Jerusalem, and everything that is written of the Son of Man by the prophets will be accomplished. For He will be delivered to the Gentiles, and will be mocked and shamefully treated and spit upon; they will scourge Him and kill Him, and on the third day He will rise." (Lk. 31-34).

Jesus also said, "So, could you not watch with me one hour? Watch and pray that you may not enter into temptation; the spirit indeed is willing, but the flesh is weak." (Mt. 26:40-41).

All: So, Jesus, we now give you this hour as we watch and pray with you. We also turn to Our Lady of Guadalupe and ask her to spiritually accompany us as we proceed on your Way of the Cross.

Our Lady of Guadalupe, Protectress of the Unborn, today you walk the Way of the Cross with Jesus who appears to us in the terrible suffering guise of the unborn children who are aborted and the embryos who are killed. We ask you to intercede to Jesus with Blessed Mother Teresa and Servant of God Dorothy Day for eternal life for them, for repentance, conversion and eternal life for their parents and killers, for the protection of all unborn children, for reverence for all life from conception to natural death and for a Culture of Life and a Civilization of Love.

"Abba, Father, all things are possible to you;
remove this cup from me.
Yet not my will but yours be done." (Mk. 14:36).

Leader:
The First Station

Jesus is Condemned to Death

All sing: Were you there when they condemned my Lord to death?
Were you there when they condemned my Lord to death?
O, sometimes it causes me to tremble, tremble, tremble.
Were you there when they condemned my Lord to death?

Leader: We adore you, O Christ, and we praise you.

All: Because by your Holy Cross, you have redeemed the world.

Leader: *My people, what have I done to you?*
How have I offended you? Answer me
I led you on your way in a pillar of cloud,
but you led me to Pilate's court.

So Jesus came out, wearing the crown of thorns and the purple robe. Pilate said to them, "Behold the man!" When the chief priests and the officers saw Him, they cried out, "Crucify Him, crucify Him!" (Jn. 19:5-6).

His wife sent him this message: "Don't have anything to do with that innocent man, for I have suffered a great deal today in a dream because of Him." (Mt. 27:19).

Pilate said to them, "Take Him yourselves and crucify Him, for I find no crime in Him." (Jn. 19:6).

The Jews answered him, "We have a law, and by that law He ought to die, because He has made Himself the Son of God." (Jn. 19:7).

All: Jesus, you were scourged and crowned with thorns. Your body was ripped to shreds so brutally that even Pilate was moved to pity and said, "Behold the man!" But the crowd without pity yelled, "Crucify Him, crucify Him!" Both Pilate and his wife knew that you were totally innocent. Even so, Pilate condemned you to death.

You said that you came not to condemn the world, but to save it. (Jn. 3:17). Like a lamb led to the slaughter, you stood in silence. Pilate was an unjust judge who cowardly wanted to please the crowd that cried for your crucifixion rather than to do the right thing and release you. Although he washed his hands and said that he was not responsible for your death, in fact he was responsible because your freedom rested in his hands.

Jesus, today many innocent unborn children are condemned to death by their own parents. Their bodies are ripped to shreds like yours was. Some parents are ignorant, some want to please themselves, some want to please others. Like the crowd that was in front of you, the parents and killers say, "We have a law" and, like Pilate, they condemn the unborn children to death. But the law allowing abortions is unjust and so are the condemnations. God also has His law, "Thou shalt not kill."

Jesus, help them to follow your law and to listen to the voices like Pilate's wife who counsel against killing and not to the crowd that shouts, "It's legal." May they see the truth of abortion and behold the images of bloody aborted children with pity as Pilate beheld you.

Now pray the Concluding Prayers located on page 95.

All sing: As they yelled, "You must die,"
"Crucify Him!" was their cry.
So you were condemned to death.

Leader: **The Second Station**
Jesus Takes Up His Cross

All sing: Were you there when He took up His Cross?
Were you there when He took up His Cross?
O, sometimes it causes me to tremble, tremble, tremble.
Were you there when He took up His Cross?

Leader: We adore you, O Christ, and we praise you.

All: Because by your Holy Cross, you have redeemed the world.

Leader: *I led you out of Egypt, from slavery to freedom but you led your Savior to the Cross.*

Pilate said to Him, "So you are a king?" Jesus answered, "You say that I am a king. For this I was born, and for this I have come into the world, to bear witness to the truth. Every one who is of the truth hears my voice." Pilate said to Him, "What is truth?" (Jn. 18: 37-38).

And when they had mocked Him, they stripped Him of the purple cloak, and put His own clothes on Him. And they led Him out to crucify Him. (Mk.15:20).

So they took Jesus, and He went out, bearing His own Cross, to the place called the place of a skull, which is called in Hebrew Golgotha. (Jn. 19:17).

All: Jesus, you came to bear witness to the truth, but they made you bear a Cross. You said, "If any man would come after me, let him deny himself and take up his cross daily and follow me." (Lk. 9:23).

You bore witness to this, gave us the example and picked up your own Cross. It weighed heavily upon your shoulders and added great pain to that already caused by your scourging and crowning with thorns. You carried your Cross to Calvary where you were crucified.

Jesus, today many mothers do not accept their unborn children and do not carry them to term. They carry them to abortion centers to be killed. They may think that their unborn children are crosses, but the truth is that they are innocent human beings. These mothers are spiritually carrying you to our modern day Calvaries.

May they recognize the truth of the humanity of unborn children and not be like Pilate who said, "What is truth?"

Now Pray the Concluding Prayers located on page 95.

All sing: They stripped you of the purple cloak,
And laid the Cross which was your yoke.
Then they led you out to die.

Leader: **The Third Station**
Jesus Falls The First Time

All sing: Were you there when He fell the first time?
Were you there when He fell the first time?
O, sometimes it causes me to tremble, tremble, tremble.
Were you there when He fell the first time?

Leader: We adore you, O Christ, and we praise you.

All: Because by your Holy Cross, you have redeemed the world.

Leader: *For your sake I scourged your captors and their firstborn sons, but you brought your scourges down on me. I gave my back to the smiters, and my cheeks to those who pulled out the beard; I hid not my face from shame and spitting. (Is. 50:6).*

When John the Baptist saw Jesus coming toward him, he said, "Behold, the Lamb of God, who takes away the sin of the world!" (Jn. 1:29).

But when He was accused by the chief priests and elders, He made no answer. Then Pilate said to Him, "Do you not hear how many things they testify against you?" But He gave him no answer, not even to a single charge. (Mt. 27:12-14).

All: Jesus, we see you coming, as did St. John the Baptist, as the Lamb of God who is led to His death like a silent lamb to the slaughter. You fell from weakness on the stony ground and the earth received your blood.

Jesus, today the blood of the innocent aborted unborn children cries out from the earth for vengeance. But we plead for your mercy. Many parents think that their unborn child is a cross that is too heavy for them to carry. So, in their weakness, they fall into the sin of abortion. Be merciful to them and give them the strength to carry their unborn children to life.

Now pray the Concluding Prayers located on page 95.

All sing: Behold the Lamb who now falls.
In His silence He us calls
To a life of sacrifice.

Leader: **The Fourth Station**
Jesus Meets His Mother

All sing: Were you there when He met His Mother?
Were you there when He met His Mother?
O, sometimes it causes me to tremble, tremble, tremble.
Were you there when He met His Mother?

Leader: We adore you, O Christ, and we praise you.

All: Because by your Holy Cross, you have redeemed the world.

Leader: *I led you from slavery to freedom and drowned your captors in the sea, but you handed me over to your high priests.*

All: Jesus, your Mother's eyes looked upon you as you met. Her presence gave you great consolation. Neither of you spoke but both of you communicated your love for one another by your gaze.

Jesus, today the eyes of the mothers of aborted children never look upon them. They never meet them. They are no consolation to their unborn children but only bring the desolation of death. No love is communicated from them. May all unborn children come to birth and pray to you with the psalmist,

> *Thou art He who took me from the womb;*
> *Thou didst keep me safe upon my mother's breasts.*
> *Upon thee was I cast from my birth,*
> *and since my mother bore me thou hast been my God.* (Ps. 22:9-10).

Now pray the Concluding Prayers located on page 95.

All sing: Oh, how sad and sore distressed,
Was your Mother highly blessed,
To gaze upon you on your way.

Leader: **The Fifth Station**
Simon Helps Jesus to Carry His Cross

All sing: Were you there when Simon helped Him carry His Cross?
Were you there when Simon helped Him carry His Cross?
O, sometimes it causes me to tremble, tremble, tremble.
Were you there when Simon helped Him carry His Cross?

Leader: We adore you, O Christ, and we praise you.

All: Because by your Holy Cross, you have redeemed the world.

Leader: *For you I struck down the kings of Canaan, but you struck my head with a reed.*

And as they led him away, they seized one Simon of Cyrene, who was coming in from the country, and laid on him the Cross, to carry it behind Jesus. (Lk. 23:26).

All: Jesus, Simon reluctantly helped you to carry your Cross only because he was forced to do so by the Roman soldiers.

Jesus, today, unlike Simon, there are many who are willing to carry what some parents of unborn children think is a cross. They will help them to bring their children to life. May their parents accept their help as you accepted the help of Simon.

Now pray the Concluding Prayers located on page 95.

All sing: Now the Cross is laid on Simon,
As symbolic of all men
To carry it behind you.

Leader: **The Sixth Station**
Veronica Wipes The Face of Jesus

All sing: Were you there when Veronica wiped His face?
Were you there when Veronica wiped His face?
O, sometimes it causes me to tremble, tremble, tremble.
Were you there when Veronica wiped His face?

Leader: We adore you, O Christ, and we praise you.

All: Because by your Holy Cross, you have redeemed the world.

Leader: *I gave you a royal scepter,*
but you gave me a crown of thorns.
Is it nothing to you, all you who pass by?
Look and see if there is any sorrow like my
sorrow which was brought upon me.
(Lam. 1:12).

> *Go and learn what this means,*
> *I desire mercy, and not sacrifice.* (Mt. 9:13).

All: Jesus, unlike the others who passed you by, Veronica fearlessly stepped out from the crowd to alleviate your suffering. Mercifully, she wiped the blood from your face with her veil. You left your image upon it in honor of her compassion.

Jesus, today there is no one to wipe the blood from the aborted children. Like Pilate, their doctors wipe it from their own hands. Their parents give them no mercy or compassion. Be merciful to them and give them the strength to carry their unborn children to life.

Now pray the Concluding Prayers located on page 95.

All sing: Veronica wipes your face.
In her there is no disgrace.
You left your image on her veil.

Leader: **The Seventh Station**
Jesus Falls The Second Time

All sing: Were you there when He fell the second time?
Were you there when He fell the second time?
O, sometimes it causes me to tremble, tremble, tremble.
Were you there when He fell the second time?

Leader: We adore you, O Christ, and we praise you.

All: Because by your Holy Cross, you have redeemed the world.

Leader: *For forty years I led you safely through the desert.*
I fed you with manna from heaven and brought you to a land of plenty;
but you led your Savior to the Cross.

> *I am poured out like water,*
> *and all my bones are out of joint;*
> *my heart is like wax,*
> *it is melted within my breast;* (Ps. 22:4).

Pilate said, "I find no crime in Him. But you have a custom that I should release one man for you at the Passover; will you have me release for you the King of the Jews?"

They cried out again, "Not this man, but Barabbas!" Now Barabbas was a robber. (Jn. 18:39-40).

All: Jesus, Barabbas is released. The guilty one goes free while you, the innocent one, are sentenced to death. On the way of your Cross you fall from exhaustion for the second time.

Jesus, today the guilty abortionists go free while the innocent unborn children are killed. Their parents are weak and they fall into the sin of abortion but they don't think of the weakness of their unborn children. Be merciful to them and give them the strength to carry their unborn children to life.

Now pray the Concluding Prayers located on page 95.

All sing: Behold the Lamb who falls again,
Keeping on as only He can,
With His eyes on Calvary.

Leader: **The Eighth Station**
Jesus Speaks to The Women of Jerusalem

All sing: Were you there when He spoke to the women?
Were you there when He spoke to the women?
O, sometimes it causes me to tremble, tremble, tremble.
Were you there when He spoke to the women?

Leader: We adore you, O Christ, and we praise you.

All: Because by your Holy Cross, you have redeemed the world.

Leader: *My people, what have I done to you?*
How have I offended you? Answer me!

And there followed Him a great multitude of the people, and of women who bewailed and lamented Him. But Jesus turning to them said, "Daughters of Jerusalem, do not weep for me, but weep for yourselves and for your children. For behold, the days are coming when they will say, 'Blessed are the barren, and the wombs that never bore, and the breasts that never gave suck!' Then they will begin to say to the mountains, 'Fall on us;' and to the hills, 'Cover us.' For if they do this when the wood is green, what will happen when it is dry?" (Lk. 23:27-31).

All: Jesus, you warned the women of Jerusalem of your judgment upon the city. You had wept over Jerusalem and said, "Would that even today you knew the things that make for peace! But now they are hid from your eyes. For the days shall come upon you, when your enemies will cast up a bank about you and surround you, and hem you in on every side, and dash you to the ground, you and your children within you, and they will not leave one stone upon another in you; because you did not know the time of your visitation." (Lk. 23:42-44). This prophecy was fulfilled 37 years later when the Roman General Titus annihilated the city.

Jesus, today the parents of the aborted children do not weep for them or for their own future. If doctors do abortions now, what will they do later? Will they take body parts from killed embryos and cloned humans? Will the elderly and handicapped be killed? And what will become of the parents of aborted children and these doctors when they die? Like the women of Jerusalem, we weep for them and for their future. We pray for their repentance, conversion and eternal life.

Now pray the Concluding Prayers located on page 95.

All sing: Holy women listen to Him,
As He warns Jerusalem.
What will happen then to them?

Leader: **The Ninth Station**
Jesus Falls The Third Time

All sing: Were you there when He fell the third time?
Were you there when He fell the third time?
O, sometimes it causes me to tremble, tremble, tremble.
Were you there when He fell the third time?

Leader: We adore you, O Christ, and we praise you.

All: Because by your Holy Cross, you have redeemed the world.

Leader: *I bore you up with manna in the desert, but you struck me down and scourged me.*

All who see me mock me,
they make faces at me,
they wag their heads;
. . . my strength is dried up like a clay pot,
and my tongue cleaves to my jaws;
thou dost lay me in the dust of death. (Ps. 22:7; 15).

All: Jesus, you fell in the dust for the third and last time in utter weakness. But, you got up once again. There was no shame on you. However, Peter fell in shame from the virtue of courage by denying you three times.

Jesus, today many parents fall into the sin of abortion two, three and more times. They shamefully lack courage and strength to bring their unborn children to birth. May all parents have the virtue of courage to bring their unborn children to life.

Now pray the Concluding Prayers located on page 95.

All sing: Like a lamb that's led to die,
On the ground He does lie,
Helpless as an unborn child.

Leader:	**The Tenth Station** **Jesus Is Stripped of His Garments**
All sing:	Were you there when they stripped Him of His garments? Were you there when they stripped Him of His garments? O, sometimes it causes me to tremble, tremble, tremble. Were you there when they stripped Him of His garments?
Leader:	We adore you, O Christ, and we praise you.
All:	Because by your Holy Cross, you have redeemed the world.
Leader:	*I gave you saving water from the rock,* *but you gave me gall and vinegar to drink.*

I can count all my bones —
They stare and gloat over me;
They divide my garments among them
and for my raiment they cast lots. (Ps. 22:17-18).

When the soldiers had crucified Jesus they took His garments and made four parts, one for each soldier; also His tunic. But the tunic was without seam, woven from top to bottom; so they said to one another, "Let us not tear it, but cast lots for it to see whose it shall be."

This was to fulfill the scripture, "They parted my garments among them, and for my clothing they cast lots." (Jn. 19:23-24).

All: Jesus, they stripped you of your garments, ripping open all of the wounds of your body. They divided your garments and cast lots for them.

Jesus, today some doctors strip the skin from unborn children by abortion and divide and sell their body parts. We pray for their repentance, conversion and eternal life.

Now pray the Concluding Prayers located on page 95.

All sing: They divided up your garments
And cast lots for your raiment.
Like doctors dividing body parts.

Leader: **The Eleventh Station**
Jesus Is Nailed to The Cross

All sing: Were you there when they nailed Him to the Cross?
Were you there when they nailed Him to the Cross?
O, sometimes it causes me to tremble, tremble, tremble.
Were you there when they nailed Him to the Cross?

Leader: We adore you, O Christ, and we praise you.

All: Because by your Holy Cross, you have redeemed the world.

Leader: *I raised you to the height of majesty, but you have raised me high on a Cross.*

> *Yea, dogs are round about me;*
> *a company of evildoers encircle me;*
> *they have pierced my hands and feet.* (Ps. 22:16).
> *This is my body which is given for you.*
> (Lk. 22:19)

All: Jesus, they nailed your hands and feet to the Cross, pulling your arms to reach the pre-drilled nail holes. They dislocated your shoulder.

Jesus, today some doctors rip the bodies of unborn children by abortion. As your head was crowned with thorns, their heads are crushed by forceps. Their joints are dislocated. Have mercy on them.

Now pray the Concluding Prayers located on page 95.

All sing: For the sins of your own nation,
You were nailed in desolation.
Till you sent your spirit forth.

Leader: **The Twelfth Station**
Jesus Dies on The Cross

All sing: Were you there when He died on the Cross?
Were you there when He died on the Cross?
O, sometimes it causes me to tremble, tremble, tremble.
Were you there when He died on the Cross?

Leader: We adore you, O Christ, and we praise you.

All: Because by your Holy Cross, you have redeemed the world.

Leader: *I opened the sea before you,*
but you opened my side with a spear.
This cup which is poured out for you
is the new covenant in my blood. (Lk. 22:20).

When Jesus saw His mother, and the disciple whom He loved standing near, He said to His mother, "Woman, behold, your son!" Then He said to the disciple, "Behold, your mother!" And from that hour the disciple took her to his own home. (Jn.19:26-27).

And Jesus said, "Father, forgive them; for they know not what they do." (Lk. 23:34). The Good Thief said, "Jesus, remember me when you come into your kingdom." And He said to him, "Truly, I say to you, today you will be with me in Paradise." (Lk. 23:42-43).

Then Jesus, crying with a loud voice, said, "Father, into your hands I commit my spirit!" And having said this He breathed His last. (Lk. 23:46).

One of the soldiers pierced His side with a spear, and at once there came out blood and water. (Jn. 19:34).

Now when the centurion saw what had taken place, he praised God, and said, "Certainly this man was innocent!" (Lk. 23:47).

All: Jesus, you died on the Cross at Calvary after three hours of hanging there in excruciating agony. Your Mother stood there consoling you to the end.

Jesus, today many mothers take their unborn children to abortion centers that are the Calvaries of the modern world. There they die like you in excruciating agony. However, their mothers do not stand in consolation for them. They lie down for the abortionists who abort their children.

Jesus, you said to your Mother, "Behold, your son!" But today many mothers do not behold their unborn children, they abort them. May your prayer for them still be, "Father, forgive them; for they know not what they do."

As you said to the Good Thief, may you say to the aborted children, "Truly, I say to you, today you will be with me in Paradise."

Now pray the Concluding Prayers located on page 95.

All sing: At the Cross her station keeping,
Stood your mournful Mother weeping,
Close to you until the end.

Leader: **The Thirteenth Station**
Jesus Is Taken from The Cross

All sing: Were you there when they took Him from the Cross?
Were you there when they took Him from the Cross?
O, sometimes it causes me to tremble, tremble, tremble.
Were you there when they took Him from the Cross?

Leader: We adore you, O Christ, and we praise you.

All: Because by your Holy Cross, you have redeemed the world.

Leader: *What more could I have done for you?*
I planted you as my first vine,
but you yielded only bitterness:

*when I was thirsty you gave me vinegar to drink,
and you pierced your Savior with a lance.*

After this Joseph of Arimathea, who was a disciple of Jesus, but secretly, for fear of the Jews, asked Pilate that he might take away the body of Jesus, and Pilate gave him leave. So he came and took away His body. Nicodemus also, who had at first come to Him by night, came bringing a mixture of myrrh and aloes, about a hundred pounds' weight. They took the body of Jesus, and bound it in linen cloths with the spices, as is the burial custom of the Jews. (Jn. 19:38-40).

All: Jesus, your friends took you down from your Cross and placed you in your Mother's arms.

Jesus, today the aborted children have no friends. Their mother's arms never hold them. Be merciful to them and give them the strength to carry their unborn children to life.

Now pray the Concluding Prayers located on page 95.

All sing: Mother Mary, see their weeping,
Take the unborn in your keeping.
Hold them as you held your Son.

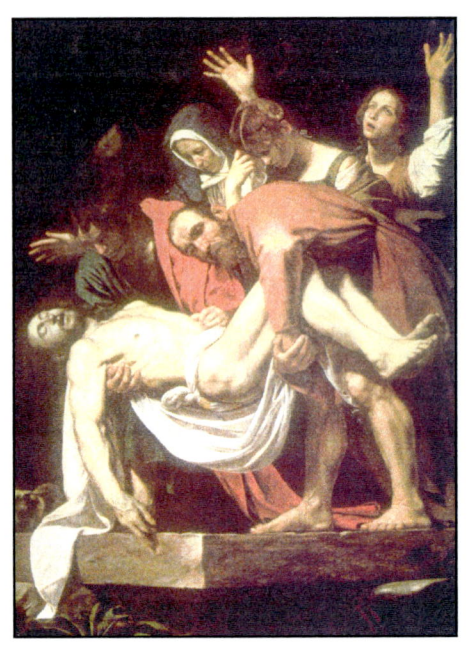

Leader:	**The Fourteenth Station** **Jesus Is Laid in The Tomb**
All sing:	Were you there when they laid Him in the tomb? Were you there when they laid Him in the tomb? O, sometimes it causes me to tremble, tremble, tremble. Were you there when they laid Him in the tomb?
Leader:	We adore you, O Christ, and we praise you.
All:	Because by your Holy Cross, you have redeemed the world.
Leader:	*The Son of Man is to be delivered into the hands of men, and they will kill Him, and He will be*

> *raised on the third day.* (Mt. 17:22-23).
> *I will not leave you desolate; I will come to you...*
> *because I live, you will live also.* (Jn. 14:18-19).

Now in the place where He was crucified there was a garden, and in the garden a new tomb where no one had ever been laid. So because of the Jewish day of Preparation, as the tomb was close at hand, they laid Jesus there. (Jn. 19:41-42).

But God raised Him from the dead, and for many days he appeared to those who had come up with Him from Galilee to Jerusalem.

These are now His witnesses before the people. We ourselves are proclaiming this good news to you that God promised our fathers He has brought to fulfillment for us, their children, by raising up Jesus, as it is written in the second psalm, "You are my Son; this day I have begotten you." (Acts 13:30-33).

Then the seventh angel blew his trumpet, and there were loud voices in heaven, saying, "The kingdom of the world has become the kingdom of our Lord and of His Christ, and He shall reign for ever and ever." (Rev. 11:15).

All: Jesus, Joseph of Arimathea kindly provided a new tomb for your burial.

Jesus, today no one provides a funeral, a burial or a tomb for the aborted children. They are just thrown away, flushed down the drain or sold for body parts. Have mercy on them.

Now pray the Concluding Prayers located on page 95.

All sing: They laid you down in the tomb,
As are those killed in the womb.
But like you they'll rise again.

Closing Prayer for Unborn Victims
To Jesus King of All Nations and Our Lady of Guadalupe, Protectress of The Unborn

Leader: Jesus told an American mystic, *"Pray for all those who have been involved in abortions. Yes, pray that they become reconciled with me. Many stay away out of pride. Others do not return to me for Satan has them bound by fear and guilt. But my arms are outstretched and filled with love and mercy. Pray that these souls are healed emotionally and spiritually. Pray for any who encourage abortion, or aid in the act itself. These too, my mercy calls. Many who submit to this heinous crime are being misled. Pray that hearts open to the truth."*

And so we pray for all victims of abortion and embryonic killing, the unborn children, their parents, the killers and their helpers. May those involved in these killings be reconciled to God and may the innocent dead be saved.

All: O Lord our God, You alone are the Most Holy King and Ruler of all nations. We pray to You, Lord, in the great expectation of receiving from You, O Divine King, mercy, peace, justice and all good things.

Protect, O Lord our King, our families and the land of our birth. Guard us, we pray, Most Faithful One! Protect us from our enemies and from Your Just Judgment.

Forgive us, O Sovereign King, our sins against You. Jesus, You are King of Mercy. We have deserved Your Just Judgment. Have mercy on us, Lord, and forgive us. We trust in Your Great Mercy.

O most awe-inspiring King, we bow before You and pray; may Your Reign, Your Kingdom, be recognized on earth!

Holy Mother of God and of the Church, Our Lady of Guadalupe, you were chosen by the Father for the Son through the Holy Spirit.

You are the Woman through whom Satan is crushed. (See Gen. 3:15). You are the Woman Clothed with the Sun who labors to give birth to the Body of Christ while Satan, the Red Dragon, waits to voraciously devour your child. (See Rev. 12).

So too did Herod seek to voraciously destroy your Son, Our Lord and Savior Jesus Christ, and massacred many innocent children in the process. (See Mt. 2).

So today many innocent unborn children are massacred in the attack upon human life and upon the Church, the Body of Christ.

Like Rachel, we lament and we bewail the children who are no more. (See Mt. 2:18). Mother of the Innocents, we praise God in you for His gifts to you of your Immaculate Conception (conceived without original sin), your freedom from actual sin; your fullness of grace, your Motherhood of God and of the Church, your Perpetual Virginity and your Assumption body and soul into Heaven.

We pray for all abortion centers throughout the world. We ask you to intercede with God to convert all abortion centers to ones that protect and foster all human life, married life and the family, God's foundation for society.

O Help of Christians, we beg you to protect all mothers of the unborn and the children within their wombs. We plead with you for your help to end the holocaust of abortion and embryonic killings now! Melt hearts so that life may be revered!

Holy Mother, we pray to your Sorrowful and Immaculate Heart for all unborn children that they may have life here on earth and by the most Precious Blood shed by your Son that they may have eternal life with Him in heaven. We also pray for the eternal life of all killed unborn children and that their parents, all abortionists and all abortion supporters may be converted, accept your Son, Jesus Christ, as their Lord and Savior and have eternal life with Him. Defend all of your children in the battle against Satan and all of the evil spirits in this present darkness.

We desire that the innocent unborn children who die without Baptism should be baptized and saved. We ask that you obtain this grace for them and repentance, reconciliation and pardon from God for their parents and their killers.

Let there be revealed, once more, in the history of the world the infinite power of merciful love. May it put an end to evil. May it transform consciences. May your Sorrowful and Immaculate Heart reveal for all the light of hope. May Jesus King of All Nations reign over us, our families, cities, states, nations and the whole of humanity.

O clement, O loving, O Sweet Virgin Mary, hear our pleas and accept this cry from our hearts!

Our Lady of Guadalupe, Protectress of the Unborn, pray for us!

Leader: Holy God, Holy Mighty One, Holy Immortal One,

All: Have mercy on us and on the whole world.

Leader: Holy God, Holy Mighty One, Holy Immortal One,

All: Have mercy on us and on the whole world.

Leader: Holy God, Holy Mighty One, Holy Immortal One,

All: Have mercy on us and on the whole world. Amen.

Concluding Prayers Prayed After Each Station

Leader: Eternal Father, we offer you the Body and Blood,
Soul and Divinity, of your dearly beloved Son, Our Lord Jesus Christ,

All: In atonement for our sins and those of the whole world.

Leader: For the sake of His sorrowful Passion,

All: Have mercy on us and on the whole world.

Leader: Let us pray the Prayer from the Sequence of the Easter Sunday Liturgy:

All: Christians, to the Paschal Victim
Offer your thankful praises!
A Lamb the sheep redeems;
Christ, who only is sinless,
Reconciles sinners to the Father.
Death and life have contended in that combat stupendous:
The Prince of life, who died, reigns immortal . . . .
Christ indeed from death is risen, our new life obtaining.
Have mercy, victor King, ever reigning!
Amen. Alleluia.

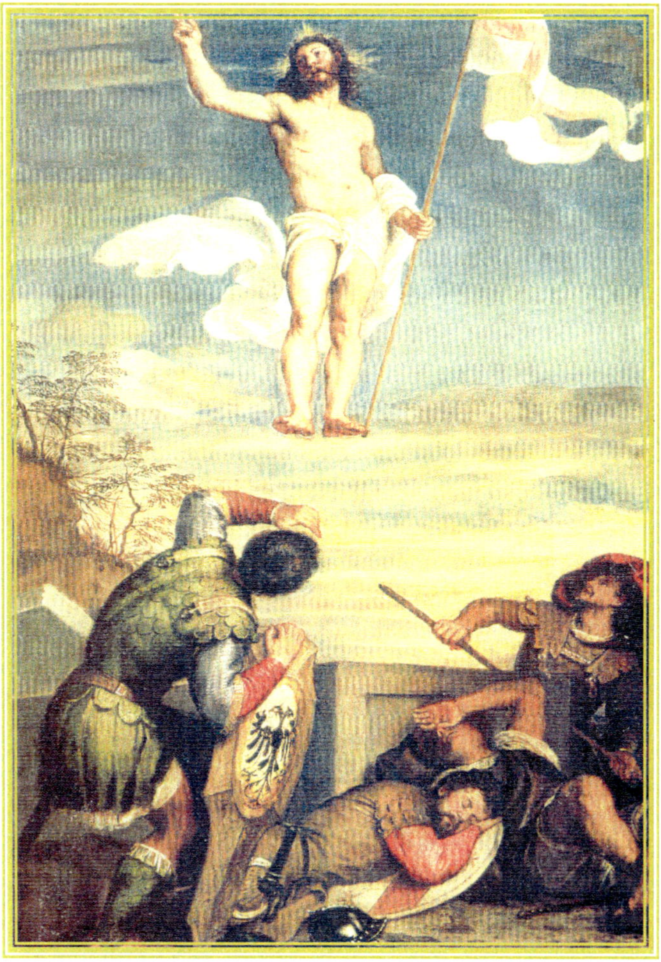

The Chaplet of Our Lady of Guadalupe

This 24 bead chaplet consists of six units each containing a single bead and a group of three beads. The six single beads signify the six apparitions of Our Lady of Guadalupe.

Make the sign of the Cross and say the Apostles Creed.

Say one "Our Father", three "Hail Marys" and one "Glory Be."

Announce the first apparition listed below and say one "Our Father" three "Hail Marys" and one "Glory Be." Repeat for each apparition. At the end say the Closing Prayer.

1st Apparition: Our Lady of Guadalupe appears to Saint Juan Diego on Tepeyac Hill and requests that a sanctuary be built there to manifest her Son Jesus.

2nd Apparition: Our Lady of Guadalupe gives Juan encouragement to continue his mission after his first return from the Bishop's house.

3rd Apparition: Our Lady of Guadalupe promises Juan a sign for the Bishop after his second return from the Bishop's house.

4th Apparition: Our Lady of Guadalupe asks Juan to pick the Castilian roses blooming on Tepeyac Hill and arranges them in his tilma.

5th Apparition: Our Lady of Guadalupe appears to Juan's uncle, Juan Bernardino, and he is healed and restored to health.

6th Apparition: Our Lady of Guadalupe fulfills her promise to Juan by showing herself on Juan's tilma to the Bishop.

Closing Prayer: Praised be the name of Jesus. May you, the Virgin of Guadalupe, the Mother of the True God, help all those who invoke you to help with their necessities. May you guide us in righteous paths and protect us from all evil. Long live Christ the King! Long live Our Lady of Guadalupe! Amen.

Memorare to
Our Lady of Guadalupe

Remember, O most gracious Virgin of Guadalupe, that in your celestial apparitions on the mount of Tepeyac, you promised to show your compassion and pity towards all who, loving and trusting you, seek your help and call upon you in their necessities and afflictions. You promised to hear our supplications, to dry our tears and to give us consolation and relief. Never has it been known that anyone who fled to your protection, implored your help, or sought your intercession, either for the common welfare, or in personal anxieties, was left unaided.

Inspired by this confidence, we fly unto you, O Mary, ever Virgin Mother of the true God! Though grieving under the weight of our sins, we come to prostrate ourselves in your august presence, certain that you will deign to fulfill your merciful promises. We are full of hope that, standing beneath your shadow and protection, nothing will trouble or afflict us, nor need we fear illness or misfortune, or other sorrow.

You have desired to remain with us through your admirable Image, you who are our Mother, our health and our life. Placing ourselves beneath your maternal gaze and having recourse to you in all our necessities, we need do nothing more.

O holy Mother of God, despise not our petitions, but in your mercy hear and answer them. Amen.

Make of Me a Tilma
Patti Gallagher Mansfield

O Most Holy Lord, you can do all things.

Make of me a tilma,

   To show forth your love to the peoples of the New World you caused the image of your Merciful Mother to appear on the cloak of Juan Diego long ago.
   If this rough-hewn fabric could attract your attention and be useful in your plan,
   Surely a willing soul like mine can serve your purpose as well.

Make of me a tilma,

   Take from me all that would spoil or distort the work of your hand.
   May your Holy Spirit render me clean and ready to receive so great a gift.
   Impress upon me the image of your pure and holy Mother,
   May her countenance, her presence, her love be indelibly stamped upon me.

Make of me a tilma,

   In this time when pagan culture threatens to engulf your people once more and destroy human life,
   Let there be a fresh miracle of grace.
   Send your Mother for a New Evangelization.
   Upon the coarse fabric of my life, draw this portrait.

Act of Consecration and Crowning to Our Lady of Guadalupe Patroness and Protectress of the Unborn

Our Lady of Guadalupe, Immaculate Conception, Perfect and Perpetual Virgin Mary, Mother of the True God and Mother of the Church, Woman Clothed with the Sun, we totally consecrate ourselves to you and to your Sorrowful and Immaculate Heart. We entrust to you all that we have and all that we are. Hear the prayer that we address to you with filial trust and present it to your son Jesus, our sole Redeemer.

As the Immaculate Conception, you are the Patroness of America. Our Holy Fathers have called you Patroness, Queen and Mother of the Americas. Popes Leo XIII and Pius XII crowned your sacred image at Tepeyac.

Today we imitate them and address you, Our Lady of Guadalupe, as our Patroness, our Queen and our Mother and we crown your Missionary Image.

We place under your patronage and protection the Pro-Life Movement and all unborn children under your special title of Patroness and Protectress of the Unborn. Please protect all mothers of the unborn and the children within their wombs. Please help their mothers to bring them to birth and help to save the souls of those who have been killed by abortion.

O Mother of mercy, help all abortionists and abortion supporters to be healed and reconciled with your Son. Melt hearts so that life may be revered from conception to natural death. Bring us the New Era with reverence for life. We pledge to help you with our prayer and sacrifice. Please end the horrible evil of the abortion holocaust without exceptions now!

We implore you, Queen of the Angels to defend all of your children and to send St. Michael and the other angels to defend us in our battle against Satan and all of the evil spirits in this present darkness arrayed against God and the human life He creates. (See Eph. 6:12).

Holy Mother of God, Mediatrix of All Graces, save us through the Flame of Love of your Sorrowful and Immaculate Heart! Send forth your Spouse, the Holy Spirit, to bring us the New Pentecost and the fire of His Divine Love to renew the face of the earth.

We desire that the innocent unborn children who die without Baptism should be baptized and saved. We ask that you obtain this grace for them and repentance, reconciliation and pardon from God for their parents and their killers.

Let there be revealed, once more, in the history of the world the infinite power of merciful love. May it put an end to evil. May it transform consciences. May your Sorrowful and Immaculate Heart reveal for all the light of hope. May Jesus King of All Nations reign in our hearts, our families, cities, states, nations and the whole of humanity. May His reign be recognized on earth!

O clement, O loving, O sweet Virgin Mary, hear our pleas and accept this cry from our hearts!

Our Lady of Guadalupe, Patroness and Protectress of the Unborn, pray for us!

We place above your head, this crown as a sign of your Queenship. You reign as Queen with your Son Jesus, King of All Nations. May this coronation be received by you, O humble Virgin Mother, so that you will reign in the hearts of all mothers. This crown puts forever under your powerful patronage and protection all unborn children and their mothers, under your title of Patroness and Protectress of the Unborn.

Long live Our Lady of Guadalupe, Patroness and Protectress of the Unborn!

Hail Holy Queen and

Manila, Philippines. Cardinals Roger Mahoney and Sin crowning Missionary Image before two million of the Filipino faithful.

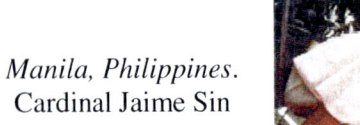

Manila, Philippines. Cardinal Jaime Sin

104

Mother of the Americas!

Cebu, Philippines. Crown and cascade of roses over Missionary Image.

Pina Blanca, New Mexico. Fr. Donen Herbe

Mexican Bishops' and Basilica's Prayers for Missionary Image of Our Lady of Guadalupe

Conference of All Mexican Bishops' Prayer

The Conference of all Mexican Bishops in their plenary meeting, on their very first day, April 8, 1991, by means of the Archbishop of Guadalajara, Juan Jesus Posadas Ocampo, made the following prayers on petition of all of the Bishops:

Mother of the True God, and our Mother, Our Lady of Guadalupe, we beg you that your trip through all the Americas be realized now beginning with the Marian Congress of the Rosary in the National Sanctuary of the Immaculate Conception in Washington, D.C., the next month of June. We know that you want to end abortion in the world and convert twenty nine million Latins who have left the Church and have taken themselves over to the sects.

Lady, help us support your mission with our prayers in order that your Missionary Image will be well received in all the Americas.

Cardinal Posadas' Prayer

The Catholic people of Mexico and I pray to God that the paths of the Journey of the Missionary Image of Our Lady of Guadalupe throughout the United States of America, become rays of Our Lady's love, care, protection and help for all of her children, particularly the unborn.

May she end without exceptions the horrible evil of abortion.

May she convert millions of hearts to the Sacred Heart of her Son Jesus and His holy Church through her Immaculate Heart.

May all pro-life forces unite under the banner of Our Lady of Guadalupe with her title of "Protectress of the Unborn."

I bless the Missionary Image of Our Lady of Guadalupe and her evangelical mission that began under her protection almost 460 years ago.

I congratulate all the promoters of such a praiseworthy mission and with pleasure I commend them to the hands of Our Lord.

Lady, help us support your mission with our prayers in order that your Missionary Image may be well received in America for the glory of God and the honor of His holy Mother!

+Juan Jesus Cardinal Posadas Ocampo
Archbishop of Guadalajara

Basilica Rector's Certificate and Blessing

Villa de Guadalupe   Certificate of Authenticity and Blessing

To whom it may concern:

May the Peace of the Lord Jesus be a fountain of inexhaustible gifts for us in the Third Millennium.

This letter has the purpose to certify that the Missionary Image of Our Lady of Guadalupe, property of Daniel Lynch, is an exact copy in color and measurements and is a replica of the Miraculous original Tilma of Juan Diego. It was made digitally in October of 2000 and certified in the same manner by His Excellency Sr. Cardinal Norberto Rivera Carrera, Archbishop of Mexico.

Through this letter I certify that I have blessed this Missionary Image for the mission of promoting sanctity of the family, solidarity of the Church in America, a culture of life and a civilization of love.

I bid farewell trusting this work of human promotion to the protection of Our Lady, Holy Mother, the Virgin of Guadalupe.

Affectionately in Christ,
Monsignor Diego Monroy Ponce
Vicar General and Bishop of Guadalupe and Rector of the Sanctuary

Monsignor Diego Monroy Ponce, Rector of the Basilica of Our Lady of Guadalupe, blessing the Missionary Image and Dan Lynch.

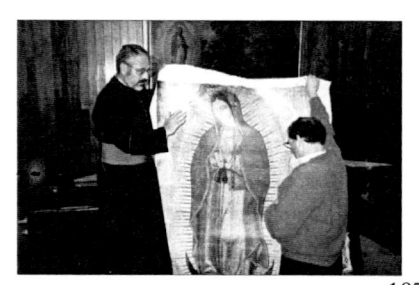

An Act of Consecration to Our Lady of Guadalupe

By Archbishop John Donoghue before
Missionary Image

John F. Donoghue, Archbishop of Atlanta, consecrated his entire Archdiocese to the Immaculate Heart of Our Lady of Guadalupe in front of the Missionary Image on January 22, 1994, the anniversary of the Roe vs. Wade *decision which legalized abortion. The Consecration was made at the conclusion of a Mass for the Unborn and has been adapted to be made by all.*

Lord Jesus Christ, Savior and Redeemer of all mankind; Incarnate Wisdom, Your humble submission unto death on the Cross revealed the power and love of the Father; and Your resurrection revealed the presence and action of the Holy Spirit. You have ransomed us from death and the power of evil and purchased us at the price of Your blood.

At the hour of Your death, You gave to us the Blessed Virgin Mary and willed her to be the Mother of the Church, the Mother of us all.

In 1531, You sent her to the Americas to be the means through which conversion and reconciliation would liberate not only the people of Mexico, but all the people of the Western Hemisphere. Our Lady of Guadalupe is Patroness of the Americas and therefore the Patroness of our country.

Before this blessed Missionary Image of Our Lady of Guadalupe, which signifies her presence among us; before this blessed image and precious gift from the Bishops of Mexico,

I do formally consecrate myself to the Immaculate Heart of Our Lady of Guadalupe.

I consecrate to Mary all that I am and all that I have.

I humbly request the fruit of this consecration be conversion, healing, reconciliation and salvation; that Our Lady of Guadalupe end abortion and all other forms of injustice, crime and discrimination. I hope that our local church will be a sign of unity and an instrument of Your peace.

Hear my prayer, Lord Jesus, through the powerful intercession of the Immaculate Heart of Our Lady of Guadalupe. I make this consecration with thanksgiving and trust and for the spiritual welfare of all Your people.

May this consecration deepen the virtues of faith, hope and charity. May it bring an awesome reverence for the gift of life and for Your Real Presence enthroned in the Eucharist. May it help us to bear witness to the Gospel and live the teachings of the Catholic Church.

And finally, may this consecration help to bring us all to the joy of Your kingdom where You live and reign with the Father and Holy Spirit; one God forever and ever. Amen.

Prayers for Life
with

Our Lady of Guadalupe, Protectress of the Unborn

Introduction

The following are Prayers for Life with Our Lady of Guadalupe, Protectress of the Unborn. They are psalms, Pope Leo XIII's Prayer to Saint Michael the Archangel, the Canticles of Elizabeth and Mary and an Act of Consecration of Guardians of Life.

A Peaceful Prayer Presence is your peaceful presence with these prayers, the Rosary and an image of Our Lady of Guadalupe at an abortion center. However, these prayers may be used by anyone, anywhere, anytime and anyhow.

At the 1993 World Youth Day in Denver, Pope John Paul II said, "Defend life. . . . Do not be afraid to go out on the streets and into public places, like the first apostles. This is no time to be ashamed of the Gospel. It is the time to preach it from the rooftops. Do not be afraid to break out of comfortable and routine modes of living, in order to take up the challenge of making Christ known in the modern metropolis."

One way to do this is to use these prayers as a Peaceful Prayer Presence on the public sidewalks in front of abortion centers. Over 20 abortion centers have closed shortly after such use and many mothers have changed their minds and chosen life for their unborn babies.

Abortion is a Horrible Evil

Abortion is a horrible evil because it is a direct attack against God, the Author of human life. It is a re-crucifixion of the innocent helpless Christ who said, "Whatever you do to the least of my brothers, that you do to me." (Mt. 25:40).

Abortion is a direct attack by Satan against innocence and against motherhood. Therefore, it is a direct attack against Jesus and His holy Mother, Mary.

God wants those guilty of abortion to be reconciled to Him and those killed by abortion to be saved. This will be accomplished through the blood shed by the innocents and our reparatory prayer, sacrifice, sacramental receptions and desire for their salvation.

Our Lady told Fr. Gobbi of the Marian Movement of Priests that "the love and anxiety of your heavenly Mother, and of the Church, for their salvation, with the innocent blood being spilled by those who despise and disobey the law of God, are a Baptism of blood and desire saving all of them."

She also told him that "the blood of these innocent ones cries out daily for vengeance in the sight of God and causes wounds of deep sorrow in my motherly heart. . . . Today there is a need for a great force of prayer. There is a need for a great chain of suffering, raised up to God in reparation." Similarly, Pope John Paul II said, "A great prayer for life is urgently needed, a prayer which will rise up throughout the world. (Pope John Paul II, Encycical Letter, *The Gospel of Life*). These prayers can help to answer the Pope's call.

Supernatural Battle

Pope John Paul II said, "We are facing an enormous and dramatic clash between good and evil, death and life, the 'culture of death' and the 'culutre of life.'" (Pope John Paul II, Encycical Letter, *The Gospel of Life*).

We are involved in a supernatural battle to end abortion in which we must use the reparatory supernatural weapons of prayer, sacrifice and the sacraments. "Our battle is not against human forces but against . . . the rulers of this world of darkness, the evil spirits in regions above." (Eph. 6:12). "This kind does not leave but by prayer and fasting." (Mt. 17-21). Pope John Paul II said, "Jesus Himself has shown us by His own example that prayer and fasting are the first and most effective weapons against the forces of evil (cf Mk. 9:29). Let us therefore discover anew the humility and the courage to pray and fast so that power from on high will break down the walls of lies and deceit." (Pope John Paul II, Encycical Letter, *The Gospel of Life*).

Brooklyn Bishop Thomas Daily said, "We can never be complacent about abortion. It's so evil, really, that only God can change it. As the

Gospel tells us, abortion is the sort of evil that can only be cast out by prayer and fasting."

"When we're talking about abortion, we're talking about Satan, we're talking about utter evil. Only God can really stop it. Only He can turn hearts around and change people's view of reality."

Abortion will end and conversions will come only through a moral miracle brought by the divine intervention of God through Our Lady's intercession and our use of God's supernatural weapons. A moral miracle exceeds human capabilities and is caused directly by God. We are His agents in causing this moral miracle in union with Our Lady of Guadalupe.

Cenacles of Total Consecration

As we engage in this supernatural battle, Our Lady wants to form us into her "combat units" in prayer cenacles. Our prayer cenacles will empower us to engage in apostolic activities to end abortion and bring conversions as the apostles brought conversions after the Pentecost experience in their cenacle with Our Lady. (See Acts 2:41). In these Cenacles of the Immaculate Heart of Mary, she will form us through our Total Consecration into the likeness of her Son. Then we will have the strength to march forth under her banner in apostolic activity to end abortion and bring conversions.

As we go forth under her banner as Our Lady of Guadalupe, we will have no better guide than St. Louis de Montfort's *True Devotion*. This book is available from our apostolate along with Cenacle Formation Packages. They teach the Total Consecration to the Immaculate Heart of Mary. This is the consecration personally made by Pope John Paul II and recommended by him to us. His motto was "Totus Tuus" which means "totally yours." May we follow his example.

Peaceful Prayer Presence

We recommend the apostolic activity of a lawful, peaceful, prayerful presence at abortion centers. These prayers will help you to form this prayerful presence in imitation of Our Lady who stood in prayer at the feet of her innocent crucified Son. Your presence is the last barrier between the unborn child's life and death. It is good for you to be there!

At the 1993 World Youth Day in Denver, Pope John Paul II said, "If you want equal justice for all, lasting justice and peace, America: Defend life. America needs much prayer . . . lest it lose its soul. Do not be afraid to go out on the streets and into public places, like the first apostles. . . ."

"America, defend life so that you may live in peace and harmony. Woe to you if you do not succeed in defending life."

This Prayer Service is an effective way to respond to the Pope's call. Many Bishops have led this or similar prayer services at abortion centers including Bishops Daily, McDonald, Montrose, Pearce, Sullivan, Vaughan and Cardinal Bevilacqua.

The Prayer Service is imitative of the Blessed Mother who stood in prayer at the feet of her crucified Son on Calvary. Jesus is re-crucified daily at abortion centers that are the Calvaries of the modern world.

Our Lady told Fr. Gobbi, "On the Calvary of this century, Jesus is continually crucified and put to death in the millions of innocent babies, who are snatched from life while they are still in the wombs of their mothers . . . ."
"Recite the holy Rosary with love and with confidence. With this prayer, made by you together with me, you are able to influence all human events, and even the future events which are awaiting you. With this prayer, you can possess the gift of a change of heart and you can obtain the much-desired gift of peace."

The recitation of the Rosary and the psalms, prayers, and hymns of this Prayer Service will bring graces at the abortion centers to change hearts and to convert abortionists, their helpers and mothers and to help to end abortion. Our apostolate has available 2' x 3' laminated full images of Our Lady of Guadalupe that are suitable to carry to the abortion centers in procession and to display them there. If trained sidewalk counselors are present, they should try to legally and peacefully educate the mothers and offer them help to give birth. The entire presence should be in peaceful, prayerful reparation.

Joan Andrews Bell, a sacrificial Rescuer of the unborn, said, "These little ones dying are intricately connected with the sufferings and death of Our Savior. There is a bond here that must not be overlooked. All the political action, educating, donation of funds, demonstrations, alternative work, important and necessary as these are, do not make up for an absence at the death scene. Thus, let me beg you to view your presence at the killing center in your area as the place where God wants you to be. . . . We may not be able to save their lives, but can we not plead on their behalf? And should they die, as usually happens (God, forgive us!) let us lift up our hearts to God Almighty on their behalf . . . it will be the only human love they will know on this earth."

Our Lady of Guadalupe claimed Tepeyac Hill for herself from Tonantzin, the false mother goddess. A hill that was used for false sacrifice was converted to one that was used to revere life through the intercession of the Mother of the Americas. She said, "Here I will demonstrate all my love and my protection to the people." In the same way, she can convert abortion centers to places where life is revered and demonstrate there her help and protection. But we have to be there to help her!

Some people mistakenly believe that it's illegal or unwise to pray near an abortion center. On the contrary, it is good to be there just as Our Lady stood in prayer before the Cross of her dying Son. We should imitate her at these Calvaries of the modern world.

So long as you are peacefully on public property, do not block access or harass people, avoid confrontation and obey all laws, court and police orders, if any, you have a constitutional and moral right to participate in a lawful, peaceful prayer presence, as suggested.

Former abortionists who have converted attest to the powerful effect of such a prayer presence. Countless children are alive today, as their mothers attest, because someone loved both of them enough to be there for them in their hour of need.

Your presence at the abortion centers is the last line of hope for the unborn children and their mothers. Your prayers and your practice of the spiritual and corporal works of mercy of instructing the ignorant, counseling the doubtful, comforting the sorrowful, feeding the hungry and sheltering the homeless are their only hope.

Mother Teresa said to President Clinton and other American leaders at the National Prayer Breakfast, "If we remember that God loves us, and that we can love others as He loves us, then America can become a sign of peace for the world. From here, a sign of care for the weakest of the weak - the unborn child - must go out to the world." Let us be that sign!

May we do our utmost to help Our Lady of Guadalupe to end abortion and convert millions as we go forth together under her banner to bring a Culture of Life and a civilization of love. May our words and actions proclaim the light of Christ to the whole world and help to fulfill Pope John Paul II's prophecy that "the light of the Gospel of Christ will shine out over the whole world by means of the Miraculous Image of His Mother."

Praying the Rosary at Masonic Hall Peaceful Prayer Presence.

The faithful praying at a Peaceful Prayer Presence with The Missionary Image of Our Lady of Guadalupe at an abortion center.

Cardinal Bevilacqua (extreme left) praying the Rosary at a Peaceful Prayer Presence with The Missionary Image of Our Lady of Guadalupe at an abortion center.

The Prayer Service

It is good to begin the Prayer Service with a Mass. After the Mass the priest can expose the Blessed Sacrament and those who wish may stay in adoration while the others process to the abortion center, recite the Rosary and begin the Prayer Service after their arrival. After the Prayer Service, the group can process back to the church for concluding Benediction.

Religious communities, young children, the sick and elderly can be asked to support the Prayer Service with their prayers and sacrifices.

The Prayer Service is not a protest or demonstration. It is a legal, peaceful and prayerful presence. It may be wise to notify the police of your plans in advance and to advertise in the media and through flyers and bulletins.

Neither the Prayer Service nor the procession should employ any signs or images except crucifixes, images of Our Lady of Guadalupe and signs which say, "We will help you to give birth!" Don't socialize with each other or argue with opponents. Just follow the Leader and pray in UNISON. The Prayer Service can also be used for other evangelistic missions for other intentions at other places.

The Leader should have a sufficient quantity of this book, a crucifix, an image of Our Lady of Guadalupe, holy water and blessed salt. The books should be distributed to all before the Prayer Service.

The format of the Prayer Service consists of an optional celebration of Mass, adoration, procession and Benediction. The prayers of the Prayer Service should be said in UNISON followed by the sprinkling of the holy water and blessed salt; Canticles, Rosaries and hymns. The Prayer Service should conclude with the Act of Consecration of Guardians of Life.

The scriptural prayers may be said in full or, if there is not enough time, pray only the bold type portions. The scriptural prayers consist of scriptural readings which extol the Word of God which gives power and authority over Satan and executes God's sentence to crush his head.

The Prologue - The Word of God

In the name of the Father, and of the Son and of the Holy Spirit.

Jn. 1

1 In the beginning was **the Word**; the Word was in God's presence; and the Word was God. 2 He was present to God in the beginning. 3Through him all things came into being, and apart from him nothing came to be. 4 Whatever came to be in him, found life, life for the light of men. 5 The light, **shines on in darkness a darkness that did not overcome it.**

Is. 55

10 For just as from the heavens the rain and snow come down and do not return there till they have watered the earth, making it fertile and fruitful, giving seed to him who sows and bread to him who eats, 11 so shall **my word** be that **goes forth from my mouth**; it shall not return to me void, but shall do my will, **achieving the end for which I sent it.**

Is. 11

4 He shall strike the ruthless with the rod of his mouth, and with the breath of his lips he shall slay the wicked.

Jer. 23

29 **Is not my word like fire,** says the LORD, like a hammer shattering rocks?

Heb. 4

12 **Indeed, God's word is living and effective, sharper than any two-edged sword.** It penetrates and divides soul and spirit, joints and marrow; it judges the reflections and thoughts of the heart. 13 Nothing is concealed from him; all lies bare and exposed to the eyes of him to whom we must render an account.

Rev. 1

12 I turned around to see whose voice it was that spoke to me. When I did so I saw seven lampstands of gold, 13 and among the lampstands One like a Son of Man wearing an ankle-length robe, with

a sash of gold about his breast. 14 The hair of his head was as white as snow-white wool and his eyes blazed like fire. 15 His feet gleamed like polished brass refined in a furnace, and his voice sounded like the roar of rushing waters. 16 In his right hand he held seven stars. **A sharp, two-edged sword came out of his mouth,** and his face shone like the sun at its brightest.

17 When I caught sight of him I fell down at his feet as though dead. He touched me with his right hand and said: "There is nothing to fear. I am the First and the Last 18 and the One who lives."

Eph. 6
10 Finally, draw your strength from the Lord and his mighty power. 11 Put on the armor of God so that you may be able to stand firm against the tactics of the devil. 12 Our battle is not against human forces but against the principalities and powers, the rulers of this world of darkness, the evil spirits in regions above. 13 You must put on the armor of God if you are to resist on the evil day; do all that your duty requires, and hold your ground. 14 Stand fast, with the truth as the belt around your waist, justice as your breastplate, 15 and zeal to propagate the gospel of peace as your footgear. 16 In all circumstances hold faith up before you as your shield; it will help you extinguish the fiery darts of the evil one. 17 **Take** the helmet of salvation and **the sword of the spirit, the word of God.**

18 At every opportunity pray in the Spirit, using prayers and petitions of every sort. Pray constantly and attentively for all in the holy company. 19 **Pray for me that God may put his word on my lips,** that I may courageously make known the mystery of the gospel - 20 that mystery for which I am an ambassador in chains. Pray that I may have courage to proclaim it as I ought.

Power and Authority Over Satan

Lk. 9

1 **Jesus** now called the Twelve together and **gave them power and authority to overcome all demons** and to cure diseases. 2 He sent them forth to proclaim the reign of God and heal the afflicted.

Lk. 10

17 The seventy-two returned in jubilation saying, "Master, even the demons are subject to us in your name."18 **He said** in reply: **"I watched Satan fall from the sky like lightning.** 19 See what I have done; **I have given you power to tread on snakes and scorpions and all the forces of the enemy, and nothing shall ever injure you.** 20 Nevertheless, do not rejoice so much in the fact that the devils are subject to you as that your names are inscribed in heaven."

Mk. 16

15 Then he told them: "Go into the whole world and proclaim the good news to all creation. 16 The man who believes in it and accepts Baptism will be saved; the man who refuses to believe in it will be condemned. 17 Signs like these will accompany those who have professed their faith: **they will use my name to expel demons**, they will speak entirely new languages, 18 they will be able to handle serpents, they will be able to drink deadly poison without harm, and the sick upon whom they lay their hands will recover."

Mt. 28

20 "Teach them to carry out everything I have commanded you. **And know that I am with you always, until the end of the world!"**

The Sentence Imposed upon Satan

Gn. 3

14 **Then the LORD God said to the serpent:** "Because you have done this, you shall be banned from all the animals and from all the wild creatures; on your belly you shall crawl, and dirt shall you eat all the days of your life. 15 **I will put enmity between you and the woman, (Mary) and between your offspring and hers; (Jesus Christ) He will strike at your head**, while you strike at his heel."

The Execution of the Sentence

Ps. 149

4 For the LORD loves his people, and he adorns the lowly with victory. 5 **Let the faithful exult in glory**; let them sing for joy upon their couches; 6 let the high praises of God be in their throats. **And let two-edged swords be in their hands (i.e. the Word of God):** 7 to execute vengeance on the nations, punishments on the peoples; 8 To bind their kings with chains, their nobles with fetters of iron; 9 **To carry out the sentence pre-ordained (i.e. to strike Satan's head from Genesis 3:15)**. This honor is for all his faithful. Alleluia.

Is. 14

12 How have you fallen from the heavens, O morning star, son of the dawn (like Satan)! **How are you cut down to the ground**, you who mowed down the nations! 13 You said in your heart: "I will scale the heavens; above the stars of God I will set up my throne; I will take my seat on the Mount of Assembly, in the recesses of the North. 14 I will ascend above the tops of the clouds; I will be like the Most High!" 15 Yet **down to the nether world you go to the recesses of the pit!**

Phil. 2

5 Your attitude must be that of Christ: 6 Though he was in the form of God, he did not deem equality with God something to be grasped at. 7 Rather, he emptied himself and took the form of a slave, being born in the likeness of men. He was known to be of human estate, 8 and it was thus that he humbled himself, obediently accepting even death, death on a cross! 9 Because of this, God highly exalted him and bestowed on him the name above every other name, 10 **so that at Jesus' name every knee must bend in the heavens, on the earth, and under the earth, 11 and every tongue proclaim to the glory of God the Father: JESUS CHRIST IS LORD!**

Dn. 3

41 And now we follow you with our whole heart, we fear you and we pray to you. 42 Do not let us be put to shame, but deal with us in your kindness and great mercy. 43 Deliver us by your wonders, and bring glory to your name, O Lord: **44 Let all those be routed who inflict evils on your servants; Let them be shamed and powerless, and**

their strength broken; 45 Let them know that you alone are the
Lord God, glorious over the whole world."

Psalm 2
The Universal Reign of the Messiah

1. Why do the nations rage
    and the peoples utter folly?
2. The kings of the earth rise up,
    and the princes conspire together
    against the LORD and against his anointed:
3. "Let us break their fetters
    and cast their bonds from us!"
4. He who is throned in heaven laughs;
    the LORD derides them.
5. Then in anger he speaks to them;
    he terrifies them in his wrath:
6. "I myself have set up my king
    on Zion, my holy mountain."
7. I will proclaim the decree of the LORD:
    the LORD said to me, "You are my son;
    this day I have begotten you.
8. Ask of me
    and **I will give you the nations for an inheritance
    and the ends of the earth for your possession.**
9. **You shall rule them with an iron rod;
    you shall shatter them like an earthen dish."**
10. And now, O kings, give heed;
    take warning you rulers of the earth.
11. **Serve the LORD** with fear,
    and rejoice before him;
    with trembling pay homage to him,
    **Lest he be angry and you perish from the way,
    when his anger blazes suddenly.**
    Happy are all who take refuge in him!

Psalm 7
An appeal to the Divine Judge

2. O LORD my God, in you I take refuge;
    save me from all my pursuers and rescue me,
3. Lest I become like the lion's prey.
    To be torn to pieces, with no one to rescue me.
7. **Rise up, O LORD, in your anger;**
    rise against the fury of my foes;
    wake to the judgment you have decreed (i.e. to crush
    Satan's head (Gn 3:15).
8. Let the assembly of the peoples surround you;
    above them on high be enthroned
9. (The LORD judges the nations.)
    Do me justice, O LORD, because I am just,
    and because of the innocence that is mine,
10. Let the malice of the wicked come to an end,
    but sustain the just, O searcher of heart and soul, O just God.
11. A shield before me is God,
    who saves the upright of heart;
12. A just judge is God,
    a God who punishes day by day.
13. Unless they be converted,
    God will sharpen his sword;
    he will bend and aim his bow,
14. Prepare his deadly weapons against them,
    and use fiery darts for arrows.
15. He who conceived iniquity and was pregnant with mischief,
    brings forth failure.
16. He has opened a hole,
    he has dug it deep
    but he falls into the pit which he has made.
17. His mischief shall recoil upon his own head;
    upon the crown of his head his violence shall rebound.
18. I will give thanks to the LORD for his justice
    and sing praise to the name of the LORD most High.

Psalm 1
True Happiness

1. Happy the man who follows not the counsel of the wicked;
    nor walks in the way of sinners,
    nor sits in the company of the insolent.
  But delights in the law of the LORD
    and meditates on his law day and night.
2. He is like a tree planted near running water,
    that yields its fruit in due season
    and whose leaves never fade. (Whatever he does, prospers.)
3. Not so **the wicked**, not so;
    they **are like chaff which the wind drives away.**
5. **Therefore in judgment the wicked shall not stand,**
    nor shall sinners, in the assembly of the just.
6. For the LORD watches over the way of the just,
    but the way of the wicked vanishes.

Psalm 33
Praise of the Lord's Power and Providence

8. Let all the earth fear the LORD;
    let all who dwell in the world revere him.
9. For he spoke, and it was made;
    he commanded, and it stood forth.
10. **The LORD brings to nought the plans of nations;**
    he foils the designs of peoples.
11. But the plan of the LORD stands forever;
    the design of his heart, through all generations.
12. Happy the nation whose God is the LORD,
    the people he has chosen for his own inheritance.
16. A king is not saved by a mighty army,
    nor is a warrior delivered by great strength.
17. Useless is the horse for safety;
    great though its strength, it cannot provide escape.
18. But see, the eyes of the LORD are upon those who fear him,
    upon those who hope for his kindness.
19. To deliver them from death
    and preserve them in spite of famine.

20. Our Soul waits for the LORD,
>   who is our help and our shield,
21. For in him our hearts rejoice;
>   in his holy name we trust.
22. May your kindness, O LORD, be upon us
>   who have put our hope in you.

Psalm 52
Deceitful Tongue

3. Why do you glory in evil,
>   you champion of infamy?
4. All the day you plot harm;
>   your tongue is like a sharpened razor,
>   you practiced deceiver!
5. You love evil rather than good,
>   falsehood rather than honest speech.
6. You love all that means ruin,
>   you of the deceitful tongue!
7. **God himself shall demolish you;**
>   **forever he shall break you;**
>   he shall pluck you from your tent,
>   and uproot you from the land of the living.
8. The just shall look on with awe
>   then they shall laugh at him:
9. "This is the man who made not God the source of his strength,
>   but put his trust in his great wealth,
>   and his strength in harmful plots."
10. But I, like a green olive tree in the house of God,
>   trust in the kindness of God forever and ever.
11. I will thank you always
>   for what you have done,
>   and proclaim the goodness of your name
>   before your faithful ones.

Psalm 68
God's Triumphal Procession

2. **God arises;**
    his enemies are scattered,
    and those who hate him flee before him.
3. **As smoke is driven away, so are they driven;**
    as wax melts before the fire,
    so the wicked perish before God.
4. **But the just rejoice and exult before God;**
    they are glad and rejoice. (Repeat above twice more).
5. Sing to God, chant praise to his name,
    extol him who rides upon the clouds,
    whose name is the LORD;
    exult before him.
6. The father of orphans and the defender of widows
    is God in his holy dwelling.
7. God gives a home to the forsaken;
    he leads forth prisoners to prosperity;
    only rebels remain in the parched land.
8. O God, when you went forth at the head of your people,
    when you marched through the wilderness,
9. the earth quaked;
    it rained from heaven at the presence of God,
    at the presence of God,
    the God of Israel, the One of Sinai.
10. A bountiful rain you showered down,
    O God, upon your inheritance;
    you restored the land when it languished;
11. Your flock settled in it;
    in your goodness,
    O God, you provided it for the needy.
12. The Lord gives the word;
    women bear the glad tidings,
    a vast army:
13. "Kings and their hosts are fleeing,
    fleeing, and the household shall divide the spoils.
14. Though you rested among the sheepfolds,
    the wings of the dove shone with silver,
    and her pinions with a golden hue.

15. While the Almighty dispersed the kings there,
    snow fell on Zalmon."
16. High the mountains of Bashan;
    rugged the mountains of Bashan
17. Why look you jealously, you rugged mountains,
    at the mountain God has chosen for his throne,
    where the LORD himself will dwell forever?
18. The chariots of God are myriad, thousands on thousands;
    the Lord advances from Sinai to the sanctuary.
19. You have ascended on high,
    taken captives, received men as gifts - even rebels;
    the LORD God enters his dwelling.
20. Blessed day by day be the Lord, who bears our burdens;
    God, who is our salvation.
21. God is a saving God for us;
    the LORD, my Lord, controls the passageways of death.
22. **Surely God crushes the heads of his enemies,**
    the hairy crowns of those who stalk about in their guilt.
23. The LORD said: "I will fetch them back from Bashan;
    I will fetch them back from the depths of the sea,
24. So that you will bathe your feet in blood;
    the tongues of your dogs will have their share of your enemies."
25. They view your progress, O God,
    the progress of you God, my King, into the sanctuary;
26. The singers lead, the minstrels follow,
    in their midst the maidens play on timbrels.
27. In your choirs bless God;
    bless the LORD, you of Isreal's wellspring!
28. There is Benjamin, the youngest, leading them;
    the princes of Judah in a body,
    the princes of Zebulun, the princes of Naphtali.
29. **Show forth, O God, your power,**
    the power, O God, with which you took our part;
30. For your temple in Jerusalem
    let the kings bring you gifts.
31. Rebuke the wild beast of the reeds,
    the herd of strong bulls and the bullocks, the nations.
    Let them prostrate themselves with bars of silver;
    scatter the peoples who delight in war.

32. Let nobles come from Egypt;
    let Ethiopia extend its hands to God.
33. You kingdoms of the earth, sing to God,
    chant praise to the Lord
34. who rides on the heights of the ancient heavens.
    Behold, his voice resounds, the voice of power.
35. "Confess the power of God!"
    Over Israel in his majesty;
    his power is in the skies.
36. **Awesome in his sanctuary is God,**
    the God of Israel;
    he gives power and strength to his people.
    Blessed be God!

Psalm 9
Thanksgiving for the Overthrow of Hostile Nations

2. I will give thanks to you, O LORD, with all my heart;
   I will declare all your wondrous deeds.
3. I will be glad and exult in you;
   I will sing praise to your name, Most High,
4. **Because my enemies are turned back,**
   overthrown and destroyed before you.
5. For you upheld my right and my cause,
   seated on your throne, judging justly.
6. **You rebuked the nations and destroyed the wicked;**
   their name you blotted out forever and ever.
7. **The enemies are ruined completely forever;**
   the remembrance of the cities you uprooted has perished.
16. The nations are sunk in the pit they have made;
    in the snare they set, their foot is caught;
17. **In passing sentence, the LORD is manifest;**
    the wicked are trapped by the work of their own hands.
18. **To the nether world the wicked shall turn back,**
    all the nations that forget God.
19. For the needy shall not always be forgotten,
    nor shall the hope of the afflicted forever perish.
20. **Rise, O LORD, let no man prevail;**
    let the nations be judged in your presence.

21. **Strike them with terror, O LORD;
let the nations know that they are but men.**

*Psalm 150
Final Doxology with Full Orchestra*

1. **Praise the LORD** in his sanctuary,
       praise him in the firmament of his strength.
2. Praise him **for his mighty deeds,
   praise him for his sovereign majesty.**
3. Praise him with the blast of the trumpet,
       praise him with lyre and harp.
4. Praise him with timbrel and harp,
       praise him with strings and pipe.
5. Praise him with sounding cymbals,
       praise him with clanging cymbals.
6. Let everything that has breath
         praise the LORD!
    Alleluia.

Pope Leo XIII's Prayer to Saint Michael the Archangel

Most glorious Prince of the Heavenly Armies, Saint Michael the Archangel, defend us in "our battle against principalities and powers, against the rulers of this world of darkness, against the spirits of wickedness in the high places." (Eph. 6:12). Come to our assistance whom God has created to His likeness and whom He has redeemed at a great price from the tyranny of the devil. Holy Church venerates you as her guardian and protector; to you the Lord has entrusted the souls of the redeemed to be led into heaven. Pray therefore that the God of Peace will crush Satan beneath our feet, that he may no longer retain us captive and do injury to the Church. Offer our prayers to the Most High, that without delay they may draw His mercy down upon us; take hold of "the Dragon, the old Serpent, which is the Devil and Satan," bind him and cast him into the bottomless pit so that he may no longer seduce the nations. (Rev. 20:2).

God of heaven, God of earth, God of Angels, God of Archangels, God of Patriarchs, God of Prophets, God of Apostles, God of Martyrs, God of Confessors, God of Virgins, God who has power to give life after death and rest after work, because there is no other God than you and there can be no other, for you are the Creator of all things, visible and invisible, of whose reign there shall be no end, we humbly prostrate ourselves before your glorious Majesty and we beseech you to deliver us by your power from all the tyranny of the infernal spirits, from their snares, their lies and their furious wickedness; deign, O Lord, to grant us your powerful protection and to keep us safe and sound. We beseech you through Jesus Christ Our Lord. Amen.

From the snares of the devil, deliver us, O Lord.

That your Church may serve you in peace and liberty, we beseech you to hear us.

That you may crush down all enemies of your Church, we beseech you to hear us.

St. Michael the Archangel carrying the banner of Our Lady of Guadalupe and defeating Satan. (See Rev. 12:7-8).

Holy water is now sprinkled at the abortion center by the Leader while all pray:

Eternal Father, may this holy water that we sprinkle turn aside every attack of the unclean spirit and dispel the terror of the poisonous serpent from this abortion center. In your mercy make the Holy Spirit present here and bring true health and protection and care for life, through Our Lord Jesus Christ, your Son, who lives and reigns with you in the unity of the same Holy Spirit, one God, forever and ever. Amen.

Salt is now sprinkled by the Leader on a line across the entranceways to the abortion center while all pray:

Eternal Father, you ordered salt to be poured into the water by Elijah in order to restore its life-giving powers. We pour this blessed salt onto this land which you created in order to restore its use for life-giving. May no one cross this line of salt for purposes of killing. May it be a barricade to abortionists, their supporters and mothers who seek abortion. May it put to flight and drive away from this abortion center every villainy and turn of devilish deceit and every unclean spirit adjured by your Son, Jesus Christ, who will come to judge the living and the dead and the world by fire, who lives and reigns with you in the unity of the Holy Spirit, one God, forever and ever. Amen.

The Canticles of Elizabeth and Mary

Dear Mary, as you were well received by your pregnant cousin, Elizabeth, whose unborn child, John the Baptist, was sanctified in her womb by your unborn Son, Jesus Christ, and as you gave God all of the glory, let us pray as you two did.

"Elizabeth was filled with the Holy Spirit and cried out in a loud voice: 'Blest are you among women and blest is the fruit of your womb. But who am I that the mother of my Lord should come to me? The moment your greeting sounded in my ears, the baby leapt in my womb for joy. Blest is she who trusted that the Lord's words to her would be fulfilled.' "

"Then Mary said:

'My being proclaims the greatness of the Lord,
my spirit finds joy in God my savior,
For he has looked upon his servant in her lowliness;
All ages to come shall call me blessed.
God who is mighty has done great things for me,
Holy is his name;
His mercy is from age to age
On those who fear him.
He has shown might with his arm;
He has confused the proud in their inmost thoughts.
He has deposed the mighty from their thrones
and raised the lowly to high places.
The hungry he has given every good thing,
while the rich he has sent empty away.
He has upheld Israel his servant,
Ever mindful of his mercy;
Even as he promised our fathers,
Promised Abraham and his descendants
forever.' "   (Lk. 1:41-56).

Act of Consecration of Guardians of Life to
Our Lady of Guadalupe, Protectress of the Unborn

Our Lady of Guadalupe, Ever Virgin, Mother of the True God, Woman Clothed With the Sun, I totally consecrate myself to you and to your Sorrowful and Immaculate Heart.

In humility, through this consecration, I receive you, Virgin of Guadalupe, into every moment of my life and every fiber of my being. I am assured that God has chosen you for me and recall what the Angel of the Lord said to St. Joseph: "Do not be afraid to take Mary to yourself because what is in her is of the Holy Spirit." (See Mt. 1:20).

Holy Archangel Gabriel who presented to us the beauty and virtues of Mary's soul, (see Lk. 1:26-35) obtain for me the grace to imitate these virtues and, by my example, to show others how to live, how to love, how to sacrifice and how to die.

As I receive you, Queen and Mother of America, I desire, with your help, to grow in my relationship with you, a relationship which was established by your Divine Son as He hung dying on the Cross when He said to you His Holy and Sorrowful Mother, "Woman, behold your Son!" and to St. John, the beloved disciple, "Son, behold your Mother!" (See Jn. 19:26-27).

I consecrate to you, Protectress of the Unborn, my work of protecting the sacredness of all human life from conception to natural death; my work in spreading the Good News; and my work in renewing and protecting the sanctity of the family. I ask for special protection of the Infant Jesus, of you His Mother and of St. Joseph, guardian of the Holy Family of Nazareth.

I implore you, Queen of the Angels, to send St. Michael and the other angels to defend us in our battle against Satan and all of the evil spirits in this present darkness arrayed against God and the human life He creates. (See Eph. 6:12).

In reparation I will pray and sacrifice. Please pray for us who seek refuge in you, for the conversion of poor sinners who offend you and for the salvation of all souls.

I promise to keep ever before me your instruction at the Wedding Feast at Cana, "Do whatever He tells you." (See Jn. 2:5). In doing so, I will be loyal and obedient to the Pope, your first son on earth. I am sure in my consecration to you that you will lead me on a safe and sure path to the Sacred Heart of Jesus.

Holy Mother of God, save us through the Flame of Love of your Sorrowful and Immaculate Heart! Send forth the grace from your Flame of Love to the whole human race now and at the hour of our death. Send forth your Spouse, the Holy Spirit, to bring us the New Pentecost and the fire of His Divine Love to renew the face of the earth.

Let there be revealed, once more, in the history of the world the infinite power of merciful love. May it put an end to evil. May it transform consciences. May your Sorrowful and Immaculate Heart reveal for all the light of hope. May Jesus King of All Nations reign over us, our families, cities, states, nations and the whole of humanity.

O clement, O loving, O Sweet Virgin Mary, hear our pleas and accept this cry from our hearts!

Songs to Our Lady of Guadalupe

Sung by Indian Pilgrims

At the foot of the hill
Where the roses bloomed
I contemplate the Virgin
Who captured my heart.

Mother mine of Guadalupe
Mother mine, all love,
We beg you to give us
Your benediction and peace.

No other nation on earth
Has been so blessed by God
For that the Indians of Mexico
Carry you in their hearts.

Guadalupe, Guadalupe,
The name that brings us joy,
May it be ever on our lips
With great devotion.

May you be praised in heaven
Sweet Virgin Mother of God
And on earth beloved
From end to end of our land.

On Tepeyac she appeared
Like a divine Star

She is there to be our light
To protect and guide us.

Glory to the Immortal Princess
Who freed us from great evil
And to make us happy
She crushed the serpent.

Guadalupe, Guadalupe,
The name that brings us solace
It's the name of my Mother,
Of my Mother and of God's.

Sung by Indian Pilgrims

With delight I have seen the opening of perfumed
flowers in your presence, Holy Mary.

Beside the still waters, I have heard Holy Mary
singing:
I am the precious plant with hidden buds;
I was created by the one and perfect God;
I am supreme among His creatures.

O Holy Mary, you live again in your picture.
And we, the lords of this land
Sing all together from the book of anthems,
In perfect harmony we dance before you.
And you, our Bishop, our Father, preached
Over there, by the lake side.

In the beauty of the flowers did God create you, Holy Mary!
And re-created you, through a sacred painting,
In this, our Bishopric.

Delicately was your image painted
And on the sacred canvas, your soul was concealed.
All is perfect and complete in its presence,
And there, God willing, I shall dwell for ever.

Who will follow my example?
Who will hasten to come after me?
Oh, let us kneel round about her!
Let us sing sweet song
And scatter flowers in her presence!

Weeping, I commune with my own soul,
That the whole purpose of my soul may be made known,
And that the desire of my heart may be fulfilled
In the building of the Virgin's house.
Then shall my soul be at rest there.

And it shall know perfume greater than the fragrance of flowers
And my hymn will rise in praise of the beautiful bloom
Which forms her perpetual adornment!

The flower of the cocoa spreads in fragrance.
The flower of the pomoya perfume every road
Leading to this holy place.
And there I, the sweet singer, will dwell.
Hark, O harken to my hymn of joy!

Tilma
Marty Rotella and Ed Sansanelli

One day an Indian, an Aztec Indian,
Walking on a road beheld a lovely lady,
and she said
Climb to the top of this hill,
There you will see Castilian flowers.

Pick them, gather them, bundle them,
Then bring them down to me, in your Tilma.
A mantle, a cape, a garment, a robe,
A woven cloak, a Tilma.

Imagine gathering flowers in December,
They're not in sight nor in season,
These flowers are the proof you need,
The sign you're to carry to the Bishop.

A picture of love, an image of faith,
A portrait of hope, a Tilma.
Bishop Zumarraga said, "unfurl,"
Your cloak given to the world.

The roses fell, the Tilma showed,
Our Lady for all to know.
A picture of love, an image of faith,
A portrait of hope, a Tilma.

Our Lady of Guadalupe

You are the fountain of my life
Under your shadow and in your protection,
I fear no evil, no pain, no worry.
Refrain

Here, in the crossing of your arms
Could there be anything else that I need?
Nothing discourage, nothing depress me.
Refrain

You are the star of the ocean
My boat is small and the waves are so high,
But with you to guide me, I'll reach my homeland.
Refrain

You are the dawn of a new day
For you give birth to the Son of the Father.
All of my lifetime, I'll walk beside you.
Refrain

Refrain
O Maria, O most merciful Mother
Gentle Virgin with the name Guadalupe,
On a mountain we find roses in winter,
All the world has been touched by your love.

O Lady of the Americas
(Sung to melody of America the Beautiful*)*

Upon the hill of Tepeyac
Our Blessed Lady came.
To Juan Diego she appeared
And called to him by name.

O Lady of the Americas
Your portrait we revere.
Enfold us in your loving arms,
Our Queen and Mother dear.

* * * *

She bade Juan fill his tilma then
With roses of Castille
As sign for which the Bishop asked
Her presence to reveal.

And on the cloth she had impressed
Her portrait bright and clear
That all who see may be convinced
That she is ever near.

* * * *

And Juan Diego's picture, too,
She kept within her eyes
That future generations might
Her knowledge realize.

This proof of love she gave to us
That we might never fear:
Discouragement, anxiety,
All flee when she is near.

* * * *

We thank You, Father and the Son
And Holy Spirit, too,
That You have sent Our Lady here
To draw us close to You.

O Lady of the Americas
Your portrait we revere.
Enfold us in your loving arms,
Our Queen and Mother dear.

* * * *

An Inspired Plea
from Our Lady of Guadalupe

I am the Perfect and Perpetual Ever-Virgin Mary. I was conceived without original sin and committed no actual sin. My virginity was preserved before, during and after the birth of my only child, my son, Jesus Christ, true God and true man. I had no other children and never had sexual relations either before or after His birth. (See Mt. 1:23,25).

I am the Mother of the one true God, Jesus Christ, Lord of all and one of three Divine Persons with the Father and the Holy Spirit who share the divine nature and in whom we live and move and have our being. (See Acts 17:28).

God is your Creator. He is goodness and love. (See 1 Jn. 16). He so loved the world as to give to it through me His only begotten Son so that you might be saved from the everlasting fires of hell and the Kingdom of Satan for eternal life and happiness in the Kingdom of God by the forgiveness of your repented sins. (See Jn. 3:16; 1 Jn. 9).

Come to Him all of you who find life burdensome and He will give you rest. His burden is light and He is meek and humble of heart. (See Mt. 11:28). He stands knocking at the door of your heart. Won't you open it and let Him in? (See Rev. 3:20).

In me, God finds His original creative design intact. I am the New Eve and perfectly conform to God's original plan of sinless humanity. (See Gn. 3:15). I can help you!

From the moment of my conception, as a result of natural sexual intercourse between my parents, I am full of grace. (See Lk. 1:28, 1:41). This is my Immaculate Conception. By a divine privilege, I was preserved by God from all stain of sin both original and actual during my entire life on earth. As a consequence of my Immaculate Conception, my body did not undergo corruption but I was assumed body and soul into heaven. (See Ps. 16:10-11). I am now in heaven in my glorified body in the heart of the Blessed Trinity.

Because of my Divine Motherhood and cooperation in God's plan for your salvation as Co-Redemptrix and Mediatrix of All Graces, I am by grace Queen of heaven and earth, of angels and men. (See Lk. 1:32).

Because of the sins of your Culture of Death and the rejection of God's graces of conversion, my heart is pierced with a sword of sorrow. (See Lk. 2:35).

I am the Universal Mother of all humanity. (See Ps. 87:5). I carry the pain of your sins in my Sorrowful and Immaculate Heart. I intercede with my Son for your conversion. Do not alienate the souls of the little ones from me. Do not abuse my images which represent my presence among you. If you venerate and honor them, you venerate and honor me. As I am but a creature of God, when you venerate me you glorify God as I did by my Magnificat Canticle of Praise to Him. (See Lk. 1:46).

Venerate my images and I will manifest to you my love as your merciful Mother, I will give you my help and my protection from the wickedness and snares of the Devil.

Come to Jesus through me. Abandon yourselves totally! Consecrate yourselves to my Sorrowful and Immaculate Heart. I will help you! Have confidence in me. Fear nothing. Am I not your Mother? Are you not under my shadow and protection? Is there anything else that you need?

I will hear your cries and relieve your sufferings. I too suffered as your Co-Redemptrix for your salvation. I united all of my sufferings with those of my Son Jesus on His Cross. I am your fountain of life, the Mediatrix between you and Jesus, of all your prayers and sacrifices to Him and of all of Jesus' graces to you. I am His gift to you. (See Jn. 19:27).

But will Jesus find any faith when he returns to the world? (See Lk. 18:8). I want your Culture of Death to end now! I want you to convert to God and bring a Culture of Life now! But I need your help!

Please give me your prayers and sacrifices in reparation for the sins of the world and I will magnify them for God so that His grace and mercy will descend on the earth. Then the Kingdom of God will come as a universal reign of grace, beauty, harmony, holiness and peace! Do everything as best as you can!

Declaration of Human Life

We hold that these truths are divinely revealed or are evident from the exercise of right reason.

1. God our Creator is the Author of human life.
2. Human life is unique and endowed with dignity, freedom and individual rights.
3. Human life consists of the integrated union in a person of a mortal physical body and an immortal spiritual soul.
4. Human life begins by God's creative act with the cooperation of man and woman from the instant of union of spermatozoa and ovum and ends with the cessation of heart and respiratory function.
5. God's purpose in creating human life is to share His infinite goodness in His own image. Men and women thus have the duty of glorifying God through praise, thanksgiving and in service and love by cooperating with His grace in trying to know, love and serve Him and in obeying His will by fulfilling His plan for our lives culminating in eternal union with Him.
6. Men and women were originally created by God in the persons of Adam and Eve in a supernatural state of immortality with the gift of integrity or absence of conflict between the dictates of right reason and passions which gifts were lost through their personal sin of disobedience to God's command by which death and sin have since been naturally transmitted to every man and woman at the moment of their creation.

7. All men and women have been redeemed from death and sin through the personal sacrificial passion and death of Jesus Christ, one Divine person having both human and Divine natures, who has merited for us eternal life through the forgiveness of repented sins.

8. God's will is that only men and women united in marriage cooperate with Him from beginning to end in the procreation of human life.

9. God has given men and women a total and compatible integrated sexuality including the power of cooperative genital activity which gives them the power to unite and procreate in cooperation with Him.

10. It is morally wrong for men or women to interfere with God's will for the procreation of the human race under any circumstances either by artificial insemination, in vitro-fertilization, contraception, abortion, infanticide, sterilization, euthanasia, homosexuality, masturbation, fornication, adultery, divorce and remarriage, suicide, genocide, embryonic experimentation, cloning and eugenic engineering.

11. The life of the celibate person is equal in dignity to that of the married person.

12. After the personal death of a man or woman, God particularly judges the soul and those who die in the state of grace with perfect charity will promptly and eternally join Him in heaven. Those without such perfect penance, but of good will after purification in Purgatory will also eternally join God in heaven. Those who die in the state of mortal sin without repentance will promptly go to eternal hell.

13. At the end of the world, the mortal bodies of deceased men and women will be resurrected and eternally rejoined with their immortal souls and Jesus Christ will make a general eternal judgment of each person according to his works before all souls who will see with them, living and dead, their good works, their sins and their societal effects.

14. Parents have the primary duty to educate their children in these truths and their moral and biological aspects and the primary duty to supervise, control and care for their children.

15. The state has no right to legislate, declare, enforce, support, encourage or educate anything contrary to these truths and the moral and biological aspects thereof.

Dan Lynch Productions

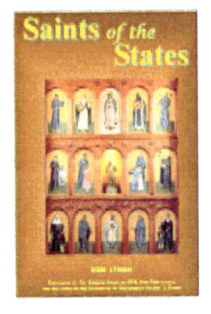

Saints of the States

A collection of short biographies of the Saints and the Beatified of America. Father Andrew Apostoli CFR, Vice Postulator for the cause of the sainthood of Archbishop Fulton Sheen, wrote the Foreword. He said, "This book is a wonderful contribution to appreciate the rich spiritual heritage we possess in the lives of so many heroic men and women of America."

Our Lady of Guadalupe, Mother of Hope!

In this video, see and hear from Guadalupe experts and the Pope in Mexico with the Mother of Hope.

Reviews by producers Ted Flynn, Tom Petrisko, Drew Mariani and Ignatius Press say: "Stirring, gripping, comprehensive with moving testimonies!"

Our Lady of Guadalupe, Hope for the World

Read the whole story from 1492 to now! Father Frank Pavone, National Director of Priests for Life wrote the Foreword and said, "This book will instruct, encourage and inspire a wide variety of people in the Church and outside the Church." Read about Our Lady's apparitions, Saint Juan Diego, signs, wonders, conversions and miracles.

Teresita's Choices

If you want to know the truth about the consequences of real choices for pre-marital sex and abortion, you should read this book!

A testimony of life, healing and hope through Our Lady of Guadalupe. Foreword by Fr. Frank Pavone, National Director of Priests for Life.

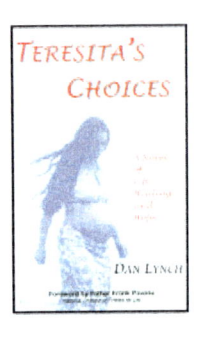

Order Form

Item	Format	Price	
Our Lady of Guadalupe, Mother of Hope Please specify English or Spanish	VHS DVD	$19.95 $23.95	_____ _____
Our Lady of Guadalupe, Hope for the World	Book	$14.95	_____
Saints of the States	Book	$15.95	_____
Teresita's Choices	Book	$12.95	_____
How to Be Holy	Audio CD	$14.95 $22.95	_____ _____
The Call to Total Consecration to the Immaculate Heart of Mary	Book	$ 9.95	_____
Praying with Our Lady of Guadalupe	Book	$14.95	_____
Prayers for Peace	Booklet	$ 4.95	_____
Prayers for Life	Booklet	$ 4.95	_____
Chastisements - How to Prepare and Pray Against Them	Booklet	$ 4.95	_____
The Way of the Cross with Our Lady of Guadalupe	Booklet	$ 5.95	_____

Value of Order	S&H
$ 0.00 - $ 9.99	$5.00
$ 10.00 - $24.99	$6.00
$ 25.00 - $49.99	$7.00
$ 50.00 - $99.99	$8.00
$ 100.00 & up	10% of order

-CANADIAN-
Double Above Rates
-FOREIGN-
Triple Above Rates

Subtotal $_____

Shipping & Handling $_____
(Must be included with all orders)

Optional Donation $_____

Total Due $_____

Method of Payment to JKMI Press:
Check Enclosed   Money Order   VISA   MasterCard   Discover

_____   _____
Credit Card Account Number   Expiration Date (MM/YY)

Name & Signature as it appears on card:_____

Name _____

Address _____

City / State / Zip _____

Daytime Phone(___)_____ E-mail _____

JKMI Press • 144 Sheldon Road • St. Albans, VT 05478
Phone 888-834-6261 or 802-524-5350 Fax 802-524-5673
E-Mail - JKMI@JKMI.com Website - www.JKMI.com